TIME COLLAPSING!

THE NEW ART OF SPEED MONEY, POWER & MEANING

ED O'KEEFE

TIME COLLAPSING!

The New Art of Speed, Money, Power and Meaning

by Ed O'Keefe

Published by: EOK Media

Edited by: Ann Maynard

ISBN: 978-0-9978280-0-9

ISBN: 978-0-9978280-1-6

ISBN: 978-0-9978280-2-3

TABLE OF CONTENTS

Dedication:

My Kids: I pray each of you find your own Time Collapsing System to Believe in Yourself, Spread Kindness, and Create Whatever Awesomeness It Is You Were Put In This World To Do!

My Wife Nola: A master at Time Collapsing, a phenomenal wife, and mother to our beautiful 7 under the age of 11.

My Parents Of 13 Children, Jack and June O'Keefe: for making us feel very rich no matter what we had or didn't have.

Acknowledgments

You quickly realize, while writing a book, how much other people have influenced you in so many positive ways. To name everybody would be impossible. so I'll keep the this a little bit short. Many of you know who you are and I love you for it.

My wife Nola: my super partner in crime and the one who makes life incredible with our family. Thank you for always believing in me and allowing me to find my own path even though it doesn't make sense most of the time.

My 7 Children: You Light Me Up, bring meaning to this world for me, and give me a ton of material to share from stage that actually makes me sound somewhat funny. This book was first and foremost written FOR YOU and I pray you take what feels right for you and apply to anything you decide to do in life.

My Parents and Family: Growing up in a family of 13 children on the Southside of Chicago has given me a perspective about life that I consider priceless. Having 12 siblings, over 50 Grandchildren and Great Grand Children, cousins (Keaty's, O'Malleys, Kalibechs) then marrying into the fantastic Farley family, all have played roles into forming the lessons in this book. To all of you,...yes that does mean the crazy ones too...I thank all of you and love you.

My College Friends: There are some people who know you best and you can connect with and whether or not you speak too often or not enough. But Sho, GC, Reg, Barta and Yes, I guess we'll include CA, despite the fact he'd show up at our games half in the bag telling everyone he could jump 42 inches. Thanks for always supporting me! Love ya!

My Coaches and Teachers: I've had some great coaches and teachers. All of which have shaped my thinking about learning, teaching, and competing. A few who come to mind that have sacrificed at some point to support me are: Peg Meyer, Niels Pedersen, Charlie Sullivan, Bruce Billingsley, Denise Lazaroni-Kavanaugh, Jen DeJarld, Therese Boyle-Niego, Bertil Wamelink, Ed McNulty, and all my NLP instructors.

My Close Entrepreneurial Friends and Mentors: The funniest thing about having entrepreneurial friends is that day coexist as a peer and as a mentor all in the same boat. The longer I am an entrepreneur the more I feel like I don't know anything about the process LOL each phase of life seems to offer up new questions and new possibilities. I'm blessed to have such good friends in my life whom I can call and get ridiculously good high quality feedback. Vinnie, Jeff, Joe, Ed C, LLoyd, Randy, and all my clients and friends.

My Athletes: I've been blessed to coach so many excellent athletes. Great human beings who helped me become better. This book was written with entrepreneurs in mind, but my goodness, every lesson can be applied directly to sports. Those lessons were forged in the trenches with you.

Entrepreneurs, Solo-Preneurs, & Creators of all kinds: This book wouldn't have anywhere to go if there weren't people like you out there making things happen. Be proud of your desire to create. Stay positive when you think you are alone- you are not!

God: For blessing me so darn much!

INTRODUCTION

"You are running out of money," my virtual CFO stated. **"You need to do something fast."**

With a bitter taste in my mouth I thought to myself: "Well, isn't that great...coming from a guy who has the luxury of swooping down once a month to read my management report with me, point out the obvious, and then bounce off into the sunset."

Then came the big question: What do I do now?

Alone and more frustrated than ever, armed with just a pen and a piece of paper, it was up to me to plan the next move.

What I did next took my company from doing $200,000 a month to over $1,700,000 in just a couple months. It was a surprisingly simple move: I changed the pricing structure of what we were selling and tweaked how we positioned our product. This increased our customer value from $130/sale to over $230 per sale.

With just a few changes our cash flow, which had been drier than the desert, was now pouring in. It was a total game-changer, and every business owner's dream!

What had previously seemed impossible (or, at best, was moving at an infuriatingly slow pace) reversed course and began to flow in the right direction in a radically short period of time. This was no fluke. Rather, external forces, internal awareness, previous groundwork, hustle and effort finally came together into what I call a "Time Collapsing Moment." And there were more to come.

TIME COLLAPSING STARTED WHEN I WAS BROKE, NAIVE, AND HAD PLANS TO CONQUER THE WORLD

The entrepreneurial world is fast-paced—no question. Yet, when it came to figuring out how to be successful in business...well, you can say my first go-around was more *tortoise-paced.*

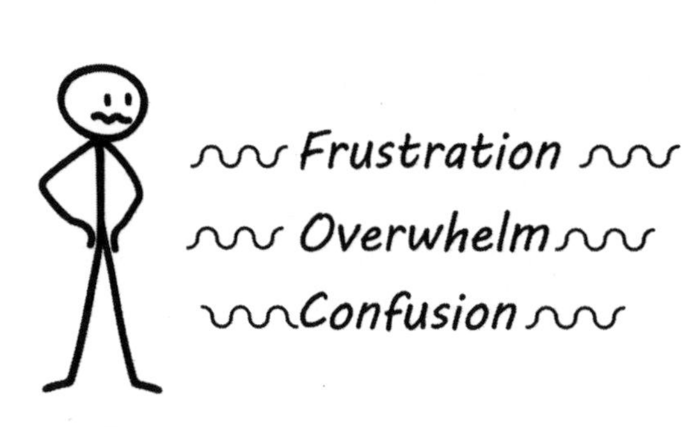

At the age of 23, after graduating from school (and nursing) I set out on my new entrepreneurial journey. I had little idea what was about to take place, but I was naively confident that it was going to be good. I wholeheartedly believed I would make a ton of money and be a multimillionaire in no time flat.

Of course, my reality didn't quite match up with my expectations. Mostly because I had no money and a small network.

The good news is that being broke gave me time to study. I dove deep into books about positive thinking and mental toughness, and felt I found the holy grail with Neuro-Linguistic Programming. I even did some deep-diving into the metaphysical, energy work, and New Age-y spheres. I was "all-in" and all over the map, but as I started to hone my understanding the foundations of Time Collapsing were beginning to come together.

Over the next few years, I immersed myself in personal development and success trainings. The first seminar I ever attended was Jack Canfield's Facilitating Skills seminar. Jack is the author of the hugely popular *Chicken Soup for the Soul* book series. He was the first success celebrity that I met in person, and a tremendous guy.

I also met Tim Piering, author of *Mastery: A technology for success and personal evolution.* Tim was the first guy I'd ever met who demonstrated the combination of a NLP (Neuro-linguistic Programming), Huna and energy work, in combination with what we might call Success 101 principles. He was a super high-level martial artist and a total badass. I couldn't know it at the time, but meeting Tim would influence my entire life path. I walked out of that seminar knowing two things: I wanted to help people. And I wanted to help myself.

THEN TONY ROBBINS CAME TO TOWN

A couple months later, I found out Tony Robbins was hosting a seminar in my area. I signed up immediately and put the tuition on a credit card. After all, when you are 23, you don't really care about money on a plastic card. I was going to be a millionaire within a year anyway. So why not?

Tony's event was unlike anything you could imagine. The music was cranking! People were jumping on chairs, hooting and hollering, pounding their chest along with Tony—and I was right there with them. Tony had become famous for his Personal Power infomercial, and I had gone through many of his audios prior to attending, but the guy is pretty damn electric in person. His energy truly fills the room.

My big takeaway from Tony's event was a full-scale belief change about my own intelligence. I was never good in school—a fact I always attributed to a lack of ability. The seminar taught me that my grades had nothing to do with my intelligence, but rather that the "one size fits all" method of teaching was a poor fit for the way I learn.

In fact people are, in general, learning machines. We learn ridiculously fast. It's just a matter of finding each person's learning strategy and then packaging information for them in that way. **Everyone has the potential to be VERY smart once they have their strategy.** With that new information in hand, my belief in my intelligence shifted from "I'm not that smart," to, "I can learn quickly and easily."

The next breakthrough was seeing Tony cure people of phobias and negative emotional trauma. I was fascinated with how a person could be absolutely terrified of something, then in a matter of minutes that fear was completely GONE. Never to return.

What was going on?

It turns out that Tony's original training for "change-work" was Neuro-linguistic Programming. According to Tony, he's added his own elements to it and now calls it NAC= Neuro Associative Conditioning.

This Neuro-Linguistic Programming thing just kept coming up everywhere I went. I NEEDED to learn it. I had a strong feeling that my job was not to sit in the seats and follow someone else who could do these skills, but to become the person who could do such amazing things.

I then met an NLP Trainer, Barbara Steppe, and the next summer went through the 20-day course to receive my Master Practitioner in NLP and Ericksonian Hypnosis. We learned everything you could imagine for fast change work in order to help people with breakthroughs. I exited the course feeling like I actually had tools, skills, and strategies that could really help people rather than just be a *motivational* speaker.

The game was on! If someone had a mental block, challenge, or emotional issue, I was eager to help...and I saw some amazing breakthroughs using these tools.

BREAKTHROUGH

An example, I received a phone call from a Dad who had been trying to track me down. He said, "I heard you can help my son."

I said, "Tell me what's going on."

He said that for the past year his 13-year-old son couldn't shower without someone standing outside the door. He couldn't sleep without a light on. "He's too afraid of being alone."

We set an appointment and, in the next week or so, I made it out to their house. When I met "Danny," the first thing I said to him was: "Hi Danny, I hear ***you can do some really cool things with your brain."***

I did this to lay a groundwork that "he was in control," that his problem was not a problem, but something that he was DOING very well.

In all the work I've done with people—from high performing athletes, entrepreneurs, to people struggling to get where they want to be—I've seen one commonality: they think they have a PROBLEM.

They don't see their obstacles as something over which they have control. This feeling creates a loss of power and makes it difficult to see potential solutions. Now, it's not always this simple—that is where techniques and strategies come into play—however, the first step is having the awareness that YOU have power to influence your situation...no matter where you are.

It didn't take long to discover where Danny's fear began: he went to a sleepover where they watched Friday the 13th, and his brain learned how to scare himself in a very intense way. All Danny needed was a new pattern, a new perspective, and this **fear that had been plaguing him for nine months was gone in a matter of minutes.**

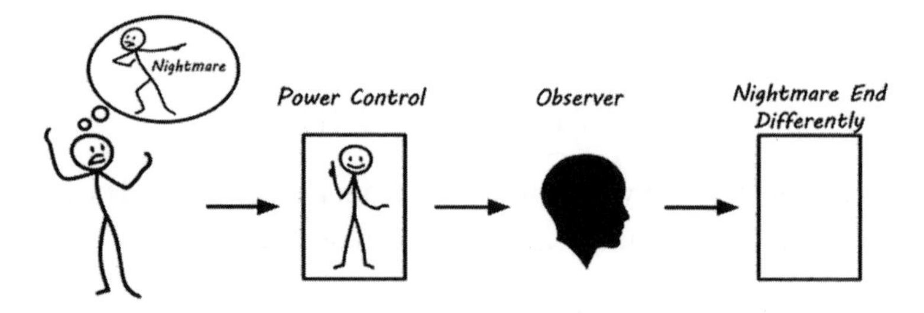

I'll go into more "change-work" strategies later in this book, however, one thing to tell you is that if it only took a few moments to change Danny's "perception" of what was going on...imagine what else is possible for all of us!

Years later, when I started looking at successful entrepreneurs who were able to create new and amazing things out of "thin air," I found myself being reminded of my work with Danny.

I began to put a lot of focus on understanding the patterns of "thinking" utilized by the success stories I wanted to emulate. I wanted to know how they thought, and how they applied those patterns to their own businesses, startups, and lives.

The bad news for me at this time was that I was still broke.

I could help people. I was a great speaker. I was setting goals. I was positive, but I had no idea how to make money.

Then I stumbled across direct response marketing, internet marketing, copywriting, and how to grow a business. I didn't know it then, but it was the beginning of Time Collapsing.

Even more, I wanted to know how I could apply similar patterns in my life, rework my own thinking, and align my own mind and strategies with the entrepreneurs who have fundamentally changed their landscape: Elon Musk, Larry Page, Peter Thiel, and so many others.

That is what this book is about:

SPEED: Most failures, ideas that can't get off the ground, cost overtaking a dream, or competition coming into the market before you do are the result of a lack of speed. Society tells you to "be patient," that "good things come to those who wait," or that it's the tortoise who wins the race. While all of those sayings are correct in a certain context, the reality is SPEED will always give you an advantage.

We'll focus on how you can predictably speed up your success in life as an entrepreneur and high performer.

POWER: Power comes from your ability to be in control of your life, shaping it into the life that you are meant to live. Power is not a macho thing or a demonstration of one's strength over another. The power I am talking about comes through one's ability to see beyond the traps that are meant to keep you average.

We'll examine those traps and identify how you can break free from the things that might be holding you back.

MONEY: Let's face it. If you want options in this world, you need to understand how the art of creating money works. I highly doubt you want to live under daily financial stress.

We will go over exactly the mathematical formula for making the amount of money you would like to make, and discuss the strategies that I've identified as the most important to creating value in this world and getting people to pay you.

MEANING: Right now we live in a world that is cluttered! Most people feel like they are doing a lot of stuff but making very little impact. Identifying your purpose, passion or calling sounds great, doesn't it? But in reality it feels much harder to pull it all together. That doesn't have to be the case.

I'll show you a framework that will set you up for success on your journey as you discover the right vehicle for you to create maximum meaning and purpose in this lifetime.

CONTROL: If you look outside of yourself to take care of your money, security, and freedom, then by default you give up your control. It's time to take it back.

My goal is to give you exactly what you need to be The Driver in your life. We are going to push the boundaries of what you believe you are capable of doing—and then we'll blow right past them!

A NEW WORLDVIEW!

Over the past 17 years, I became fascinated, addicted, and passionate with modeling the thinking and behavioral patterns, as well as the practical strategies that high performing coaches of pro level athletes and entrepreneurs who have started multi-million (or even multi-*billion*) dollar businesses!

Many of these entrepreneurs are disrupting complete industries, overturning long-established giants, or simply creating the life they want, making a good 6 figures a month living a "lifestyle" business.

To fast-forward you 15 years, I have sold well over $80,000,000 in services, consulting, supplements, seminars, and informational products since I learned these strategies and refined them for the markets and businesses I have built.

I currently advise and consult many seven and eight-figure businesses ranging from startups to seasoned pro's reinventing, repositioning, and/or on their "Second Wind" for their business career.

I'm blessed to have the opportunity to mentor high-level athletes and be surrounded by high-performing people. Humbly speaking all of this was a byproduct of many failures, many mistakes and a lot of time spent in the throes of confusion, frustration, and overwhelm.

The best part is that I am an active dad and husband, who is ALWAYS around his family. Coaching my kids sports, making lunches, putting the kids to bed, and seeing them off to school. I've changed more diapers and attended more school performances than I can count.

SO WHAT IS TIME COLLAPSING ANYWAY?

Time Collapsing is a system created by modeling high performers, real-world experience, that combines a new way of thinking, powerful strategies that work FAST, combined with lifestyle design; it's about leaping to the top, controlling your power, accelerated learning based on your unique super-power, building out your network of high achievers, diminishing barriers to entry, gaining access to any type of education you need, and focusing these efforts toward creating value to people who will pay you...FAST. By creating your own Personal Time Collapsing System, you have the potential to achieve results 2X to 200X faster than ever seen before.

This is not a step-by-step system. Traditional success and learning methods have been set up to be very linear, moving you step-by-step

along a defined "outcome/accomplishment" timeline and adhering to well-defined rules of possibility and impossibility. This, as we will discuss in the chapters to come, is not a system designed to help us achieve success. It's actually a trap that holds us back.

Time Collapsing is different. It is multidimensional and multi-directional—a map and a globe at the same time.

It is a system designed for simultaneous, exponential results, where we constantly are looking to LEAP, rather than take the stairs. The multi-dimensional, multi-directional approach allows for maximum flexibility of the path and empowers the OPERATOR (YOU) with the tools to design that path using high level skillets and thinking.

It's also an entirely different way of looking at the world. Let me show you what I mean.

Here are some of the most widely held and time-honored beliefs about success and how to achieve it:

You've got to work your way up the ranks.
You can only make it so far without an advanced degree from an elite institution.
Always be angling for a higher title.
You've got to get qualified, certified, and approved before people will take you seriously.
You need to get your name out there.
You're going to have to be poor for a while when you're getting started.
It takes time to build wealth.
Avoid risk.
Don't start until you're 100% clear on where you want to go.
Do more. Stay busy.
Once you hit a high level of success, your best days are behind you.

And finally, the big one...

FOLLOW THE RULES!

Now let's see what Time Collapsing has to say about these "sacred cows."

You've got to work your way up the ranks.

⇩

You can leap straight to the top...NOW.

You can only make it so far without an advanced degree from an elite institution.

⇩

Discover your superpower. Apply your energy efficiently. Don't waste your money or time on anything that slows down your momentum.

Always be angling for a higher title.

⇩

Results are the strongest equalizer. When you're creating great results, no one will be looking at your title.

You've got to get qualified, certified, and approved before people will take you seriously.

⇩

You do not need permission. Allow yourself to leap, create, and disrupt!

You need to get your name out there.

⇩

Get customers to chase you.

You're going to have to be poor for a while when you're getting started.

⇩

You can create money.

It takes time to build wealth.

⇩

Money is attracted to momentum.

Avoid risk.

⇩

Strategic risk is the doorway to freedom.

⇩

Don't start until you're 100% clear on where you want to go.

⇩

Answers are found in the process.

Do more. Stay busy.

⇩

Less is more. Apply your energy, time, and resources to the areas that will deliver the highest return. Don't bother with the rest.

Once you hit a high level of success, your best days are behind you.

⇩

Your biggest breakthrough is still ahead of you.

And what about that big rule? Can you guess what Time Collapsing has to say about that one?

FOLLOW THE RULES!

⇩

YOU CREATE THE RULES!

My intention is that the rest of this book gives you the tools to create your own Time Collapsing system, generating tremendous results for you again and again for the rest of your life.

Let's get started!

PART I:

The Opportunity and The Awakening

Chapter 1:

A New Face of Possibility!

"**How in the world do we do this more often?**" the young rapper and entrepreneur asked his business partner as he settled into his soft leather seat. It was their first time on a private jet and right away their mind was spinning for a way recreate the experience.

The problem was, in 1998, there were only two ways you could regularly ride in a private jet: you could buy yourself a plane outright, or you could buy into fractional ownership—both of which were seven or eight-figure solutions.

You could charter too, provided that you could get your hands on a plane and a pilot when you needed one.

At the time, all three options were out of reach for the 28-year-old and his partner. But it got him thinking: "What if I could just pay for the time I would use?"

If it's too expensive for them, two guys who just sold a music licensing company, then it's gonna be too expensive for 99.9% of the world.

They started asking, "How can we take this to the masses? How do we make this more affordable?"

As Jesse says, "***Intuitively***, we knew it would work. If we wanted to have an option to buy blocks for 25 hours to go on a few trips a year, then we knew others would want to as well."

But the big problem was, they didn't have a fleet of jets. Calling on an old favor, Jesse landed a meeting with the CEO of NetJets.

In the biggest meeting of his life, Jesse pitched him on the idea. Within 10 minutes, they were kicked out of the meeting. The CEO said something to the effect of: ***"Sounds cool, but if you think I'm gonna give my planes to a couple 27 year olds my fleet of airplanes, it's not happening!"***

After retooling their pitch, they brought in their own focus group of athletes, entertainers, agents, lawyers, who one-by-one shared why they wouldn't be a NetJets fraction, but they'd love to rent one. The deal was sealed!

In 2001, Jesse Itzler co-founded Marquis Jet partnered with NetJets to enable travelers to buy blocks of time on a private aircraft.

It didn't take long for Marquis Jet to take off selling thousands of jet card memberships each year and raking in billions. In 2010, with the thumbs-up from Warren Buffett, Marquis Jet was bought by Berkshire Hathaway.

Itzler did what I call Leapfrogging (a concept we'll be digging into in depth later in this book) and looked straight to the top of the industry to find his starting point rather than trying to work his way through ranks.

Jesse Itzler's story is just one example of the Tsunami of Success that builds from the momentum of Time Collapsing!

Around that same time Itzler's future wife, fun-loving and hardworking Sara Blakely was selling fax machines door to door by day, and learning the finer points of hosiery design by night. She was frustrated by her pantyhose.

She wanted the slimming effect that came from wearing a sturdy pair of control tops but didn't appreciate the seams that would show through finer fabrics or peek out of her open-toe shoes.

One night before dressing in a pair of white pants (which I've been informed can be tricky), Blakely lopped off the feet from a pair of pantyhose and thought she had found exactly what she was looking for—until the bottoms started rolling up. These "footless pantyhose" needed to exist, she thought, so she set about trying to construct it.

After hustling for months on everything from the design, the pitch, talking to hosiery mills, and learning the ins and outs of patent law.

Shortly thereafter, Sara, who lived in Atlanta, cold called Neiman Marcus' Dallas headquarters and said:

"I'm Sara Blakely. I invented a product that will change how women wear clothes. If you give me 10 minutes of your time, I will fly there and show you." She got the meeting.

While sitting in front of the buyer at Neiman Marcus, her pitch that was going "okay," but she had a ***gut feeling*** that she needed to do more. She turned to the female buyer and said:

"Can you follow me to the bathroom?"

Awkwardly, the gal from Neiman's said yes and showed Blakely down the hall to the restroom. Sara changed right in front of her doing her very own before and after.

The buyer instantly "got it" and said, "Sara, this is brilliant. I'm gonna try it in 7 of our stores."

Shortly after that, Oprah Winfrey's people called saying that these new footless pantyhose were going to be named the icon's favorite product of the year.

In a matter of just several years, Sara went from having $5,000 bucks in savings to being named by Forbes as the one of the richest self-made American Woman with a net worth of $1.1 Billion and one of the "100 most powerful women in the world." Those footless pantyhose were just the beginning of the company called "SPANX."

These two are great examples of Time Collapsers and, once they married in 2008, Jesse Itzler and Sara Blakely became a Time Collapsing Super Couple. Now raising their kids, while being part owners of Atlanta Hawks, along with . Jesse just finished his hysterical book, "Living With A Seal" documenting 30 days with one of the most bad-ass Navy Seals living with them and training him.

The Time Collapsing pattern is: What idea do you have or itch do you want to scratch that has not been created? Break the rules, then Leap To The Top!

TIME COLLAPSING WILL WORK FOR YOU TOO!

There are so many other tremendous examples of success: Jeff Bezos, Larry Page, Stripe, Uber, Dollar Shave Club, AirBnB, Warby Parker, and of course billion dollar launches done by companies like Apple and Tesla. They have each created massive disruption and dominated their industries. In cases like Amazon and Uber, they have completely redefined the space! And they are ALL Time Collapsers.

Their successes have left clues, patterns, and strategies for those who know how to find them!

It's ***easy*** to think those breakthroughs are created by "other people," but that's where you are wrong. There are structures of thought these entrepreneurs worked within, operating questions they asked, strategies they strung together, relationships and strategic partnerships they created, pivots they made on their journey, mentors they sought, and the list goes on. ***There is nothing about these processes that YOU cannot tap into, implement, model, and replicate to create your own success.***

Right now there are hundreds, if not thousands of examples of people just like you who have gone from **ZERO to 7 and 8 figures in less than 6-18 months while also transforming their customers lives.** And there are other success stories that go way beyond the bank account.

AN EXPERIMENT TURNS INTO 70,000,000 DOWNLOADS

Tim Ferriss started his podcast as a side hobby to give himself a break after writing and promoting his two best-sellers: "The 4 Hour Workweek," and "The 4 Hour Body." The Tim Ferriss Podcast now has had over 70,000,000 downloads and is now the driver behind what is known as "The Tim Ferriss Effect." Authors, celebrities, and thought leaders are now waiting in line to have the chance to get interviewed by Tim.

TAKE YOUR PASSION TO THE WORLD

After retiring from his career as a Navy SEAL, my mentor and friend, Commander Mark Divine, started a training program for incoming Special Operation and BUDS Candidates. That training, a 51-hour Mini-Hell Week, is now known worldwide! His main clientele are not the people he had in mind though. 80% of the participants are citizens who want to forge mental toughness and push themselves beyond what they believe they are capable. I've had the pleasure (and the pain!) of experiencing the program and I can tell you...it is NO joke!

Mark has gone on to create top-selling programs "Unbeatable Mind" and "Kokoro Yoga" and helps thousands of people! When I asked him about his business strategy, he responded: *"I've left thinking about how businesses are built and am creating things I'm passionate about, then backfilling the business."*

STUMBLE ACROSS YOUR NEXT BIG BREAKTHROUGH BY LISTENING

Vinnie Fisher has created an entire business providing back-office support for fast-growing small businesses called Fully Accountable. They send daily, weekly, and monthly financial reports so you don't have to do it yourself. Sounds boring, doesn't it? That's why he created it! Business owners kept telling him that their least favorite part of the job was managing all the reports. So, he solved their problem for them. This one business is growing by leaps and bounds!

You CAN create value in this world and get paid extraordinarily well for it!

ACHIEVE TRIPLE-DIGIT GROWTH THREE YEARS IN A ROW

My good friends Roland Frasier, Perry Belcher, and Ryan Deiss have experienced year after year triple-digit growth in their businesses, all in different markets. One of their businesses, Digital Marketer, teaches entrepreneurs and internet marketers basic to advanced strategies for growing their business online. Another one sells products to survivalists, another sells makeup brushes to women, and another sells advertising! They just keep following the clues that appear to have a pulse and follow it down another trail. If they can do this, so can you!

But Time Collapsing isn't exclusive to entrepreneurs, it happens in every field in the most awesome ways.

FIRST-TIME AUTHOR SELLS 450,000 COPIES

When J.K Rowling, who wrote the first of seven books in longhand with her daughter asleep by her side, was asked by Oprah if there was part of her that knew the success Harry Potter would be, she replied:

> "I remember once, where it was like a flash of clairvoyance.... one day when I was writing Philosopher's Stone (later to be named Sorcerer's Stone) I was walking away from the cafe. I had this moment where I suddenly thought...and was like another voice speaking to me... the voice said:
>
> "The difficulty will be getting published. If it will be published, it will be huge!"[1]

The book series went on to sell over 450 million copies, and is among the top selling books of all time!

This is Time Collapsing at it's best.

From the age of 5 or 6, Rowling always wanted to be a writer. It was her superpower. Then she had the "flash" that came to her at the age of 25 while riding on a train:

In her own words: "What came was, 'boy who doesn't know he's a wizard goes to wizarding school.' Bang. Bang. Bang. And then that was it... my head was just flooding with what's at this wizard's school."

She continues: "I don't think I had ever been so EXCITED. I had never thought about writing for children. I had never thought about aiming at that age group. And YET it was the thing I had always been meant to write!"

Rowling combined her superpower with her idea, her hustle, and the swelling momentum that came as she got into the flow of her craft. Time Collapsing works for creators of all kinds: singers, artists, actors, writers, podcasters, producers, and much more!

---

[1] "Transcript of Oprah Interview with J. K. Rowling." Harry Potters Page. Accessed June 25, 2016. http://www.harrypotterspage.com/2010/10/03/transcript-of-oprah-interview-with-j-k-rowling/.

These Real-World Examples Are Your Teachers!

In this book, my goal is to bring you the strategies of real-world entrepreneurs, investors, market disrupters, celebrities, athletes, performers and leap-froggers of all kinds who know how to navigate the unspoken trenches we all face while trying to find the key leverage points that make all the difference.

THE OPPORTUNITY TO EXPERIENCE TIME COLLAPSING HAS NEVER BEEN BETTER!

The time has never been better for you to implement these strategies in your life. **Social media, technology, globalization, Google, accessibility to sell on platforms such as Amazon, and the proliferation of new platforms/channels like Instagram, Pinterest, Vine, and Snapchat (to name a few) have COMPLETELY changed the game.**

YOU now have the capability, unlike never before to get your message out. A the same time, the customer has the ability to easily FIND YOU. The advantage has swung from BIG Business brands to the small guy or gal with a passion and ability to value!

Where in the past, an artist, author, or entrepreneur would "hope" to get their song, book, or product picked up by the "machine" and 99% would be disappointed, NOW you don't need that permission or acceptance. If it's "good," and you know how to position and market it, then the customer gets to choose it!

This gives you POWER. But before we look at the system to putting these advantages to work for you, we have to understand the TRAPS that are designed to stop you!

Chapter 2:

THE TRAP

"You wouldn't believe what Michael just did!" My wife, Nola, said via text.

"What?" I asked.

To tell the rest of the story, I need to share what happened the day before.

Michael, who was two and a half years old at the time, was playing in our neighbor's yard when he had to run inside and use the bathroom. There was just one problem: our 4-year-old was in there.

So, my neighbor said to Mike: "Just go in the bushes."

No problem, right? A boy can pee in the bushes.

The next day, Mike had to go to the bathroom once again. So, he did what he did the day before...he went in the bushes. There was just one problem: he went Number 2.

Yep, our son took a dump right on the neighbor's lawn.

The thing is: Michael did exactly what he was told. He did it correctly. He just did it in the wrong place and the wrong time.

And that, my friends, sums up exactly why most people are not experiencing the life they want. They are doing most of it correctly, exactly as they were told—however, it's all wrong. They are in the TRAP...and they don't know it.

LIFE IS FULL OF TRAPS

The worst traps in life are the ones you don't see. Or, more specifically, the ones you don't *recognize.*

You can be the hardest working, most relentless person on the planet, but if you are on the same misguided path as the slowest, laziest person on the planet, you both will end up in the same cold and lonely place. Your path will have been a trap—burning your effort, energy, and time—and you may not realize it until you're at it's end.

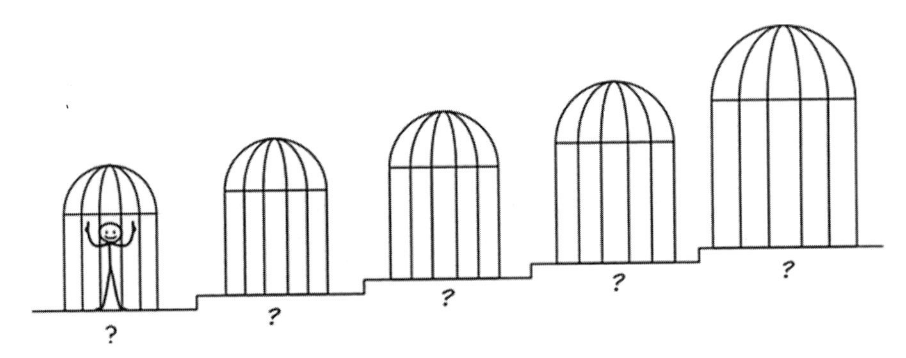

This is why hardworking, seemingly successful people feel lost, unable to understand why they aren't further ahead in life. They can't seem to fully live the life they were meant to live. They have no sense of power, no sense of control, and for many financial success or even good health seem to be elusive.

To make it worse, the paths they take to remedy the situation reinforce their traps as well.

They work longer hours, but the problem was never their work ethic.

They go back to school, but the problem was never the degree they held.

They go on a "diet" to only lose the weight temporarily, then rebound back heavier than before.

They feel "broke," some emotionally, some financially, some mentally, and some spiritually. Searching for something outside of them to "fix" the problem, **but the truth is: there is nothing wrong with them...they just don't know the rules of the game or were never given the tools to play it correctly.**

What most people don't realize is this: the curriculum of life is not setting you up to be exceptional. It is a trap designed for you to have an "average" existence alongside all the other average people out there. Keeping everyone "average" makes it easier for everyone to get along.

However, Time Collapsers see the trap for what it is—and they choose to live by a completely different set of rules.

My guess is that you share their same desire to live a life of real meaning, to know at a visceral level what it means "to live, love, and leave a legacy." But what does that really mean anyway?? Most people are just trying to get past confusion and overwhelm.

I want you to go out and feel like a badass. Confident, courageous, but most importantly equipped with tools and a worldview that works. Make as much money as you want; have the family and relationships you want; and surround yourself with amazing people who are world-class at what they do. **Become your own life's magician.**

The first key for this journey is to expose the trap for what it is.

The Trap Explained

When we were born into this world, we needed our parents, teachers, aunts, uncles, babysitters to take care of us and guide us. It was a necessity for that stage in our life.

It was during this time that the foundation for The Trap was laid. We learned that if we played nice and did what we were told, we would be called a "good" kid. This acknowledgement was important for us during this phase of life; it helped us develop **self-confidence and a positive self-identity.**

Then school started and we learned that we had rules to follow, teachers to listen to, and friends who gave us our first taste of social pressure and expectation. We learned **there is an order in life, a sequence to follow.**

We progressed from preschool to kindergarten, first grade through eighth grade, then all the way up to graduating from high school. Whether it was through our friends (or the cliques that ignored us), our teachers, or our parents, we learned that **acknowledgment, acceptance, and praise feel a lot better than unpopularity, criticism, and/or rejection.**

A sequential perspective on achievement and a thirst for external validation get established for us at a young age and can create some detrimental patterns that, if gone unnoticed, will lead to a false sense of how to succeed in the real world.

Let me take you through the traps that result from these early foundations. I will show you each trap and explain what Time Collapsers do differently. By laying this groundwork, we can then start applying these principles of Time Collapsing to your endeavor.

The Step Ladder Trap: Success is a Process

"You need to pay your dues."

"Work your way up the ladder."

"Most businesses take years before they are profitable!"

Do any of these sound familiar? I'm willing to bet they do. In fact, I'd wager that you've heard them all. The idea that success comes about via a defined "Do this, then do that" sequence has been taught, sold, repackaged in a thousand different ways and then sold to us again. This type of thinking is designed to create order—take a multi-dimensional world and simplify it—and we all willingly follow the rules. Here's the step ladder in a nutshell:

How To Succeed:

1. **Go to school, play nice, do what you are told.** Don't break the rules.
2. **Do well in school and get good grades.** Your success is measured in the marks on your report card.
3. **Look to others for feedback.** You'll know you're doing well when you get acknowledged by your teachers, coaches, parents, peers.
4. **Become a Gold-Seeker.** Get a job. Make money. Accumulate possessions: buy the house, a car, a boat. Do this for a long time.
5. **Once you retire, you can live the good life!** When you've accumulated enough wealth, you can explore your passions and spend time doing what you want. Congratulations! You're successful!

So there you have it, the path to success. There's just one teeny, tiny problem: **it doesn't work.**

If this path were actually designed to help people achieve everything they want, then why is the majority of our population floundering? It certainly isn't for a lack of good tools—access to technology, knowledge, speed, and connectivity has never been easier. It certainly isn't for lack of desire—the sheer volume of self-help books, articles, and guides to "living your best life" on the shelves of bookstores and bestseller lists are testament to our search for fulfillment. No, it's the system itself. The rules are wrong. The rules are traps.

Time Collapsers live by an entirely different set of rules. They know there is no one clear path to success (or even a clear definition of what success means). This means "success" can be achieved in any number of ways. They know that wealth can be measured beyond the bankroll, that freedom, flexibility, and speed are just as valuable. This means "wealth" is defined by what YOU value. They also know that there's no need to wait your turn. Anything is possible and it's possible right now!

Let's take a closer look at some of the other traps that may be holding you back from the success you want.

The Education Trap: Good Grades Equal Success

Get good grades and do what your teacher says = you will be successful in life. Also, the more education you have the better you will do. The inverse would then have to be true as well: if you don't have good grades, you are less likely to be successful.

Studies show that the correlation between grades and intelligence is practically irrelevant. The relationship between good grades and income is barely noticeable, if at all. But for a child there is one very clear connection: good grades win them approval and praise from mom and dad, their teacher, and their school. This in turn conditions children to strive for perfection, teaching kids that:

A. Good grades = Intelligence = Success

B. Average grades = Average Intelligence = Lower Chances for Success

C. Bad grades = Low Intelligence = No Chance for Success

However, as you read this, I hope you can see the comedy of it.

Any system that rewards "perfectionism" can be debilitating. **Perfectionism is a roadblock that prevents people from taking action, taking risk, and from creating what they want.** A much more powerful talent would be *flexibility* OVER perfectionism; *curiosity* to see what is NOT there, and *a bias toward action and results* with the understanding that you can flow to a better conclusion once the ball is rolling.

The Education Trap also gives the impression that IQ, test taking, and the ability to sit in a classroom for hours are transferrable skills that will make you a "winner" in other settings. (And, yes, they WILL make you better in a similar setting or context.) However, they ignore another crucial reality: **emotional intelligence and figuring out your own superpower is much more transferable to applying success to new contexts, environments, and ever changing social structures.**

Success is never found in an organized box, nor does it come laid out in a direct path as people would like you to believe. It's messy, confusing, frustrating, and rewarding all at the same time. Time Collapsers identify their unique superpower, how they learn best, then focus on the right knowledge (most likely not traditional)...and then find a way to apply it.

Challenge Your Assumptions: What core 1-3 skills, if developed over the next 90 days, would have the biggest impact on your ability to create value for others who would happily exchange money for it (or the results that come from it)? Do you need to go to school in order to hone these skills?

The Approval Trap: You Need Other People To Give You Permission

The approval trap is an invisible trap, rarely ever discussed, that has people looking outside for acceptance, permission, and the go-ahead to do what they want.

Getting acknowledgement and approval from someone you highly admire is not a great thing. In fact, it can be one of the most rewarding things in life. Think about it: We all want our peers and people who we value to give us the nod of approval.

However, the trap has us when we bind ourselves or limit our options and actions based on someone else's perceptions of what's important, what is possible, and what is your potential.

It's easy to end up **creating our own definition of success based on someone else's.** We end up building a framework of thinking, planning, and behaving, consciously or unconsciously to what another person thinks is right. Then we live in accordance to it.

This is one reason so many seemingly successful people wake up one day in a life they can't stand or don't enjoy. They wonder how they got there and why they aren't happy.

Time Collapsers know that seeking approval from external forces can derail your purpose at a core level. A life with meaning stems from a seed of inspiration that comes from within, and the willingness to pursue it—even without the approval of those around them.

It's not necessarily that Time Collapsers have no need for approval—they might—but the key difference is that they are aware of just how much external permission they need in order to feel comfortable moving forward. This awareness is important because the more you advance in the direction of your goals, the less likely you are to get approval from others. Once people perceive you as already being successful they no longer think you need it.

Challenge Your Assumptions: Can you think of an area of your life in which you are holding yourself back because you think someone else might disapprove or reject you? Who is that other person? Be specific.

Now, with that image in your mind, ask yourself this: What would I think or believe if I released this person's opinion or perception about my own future, capability, or potential for success?

The Societal Obligation Trap: It's Too Late To Change Your Mind

While putting my 9-year-old daughter Reese to bed the other night, she says to me: "Daddy, I don't want to play volleyball! Why is everyone telling me it's in my blood? I don't want it in my blood."

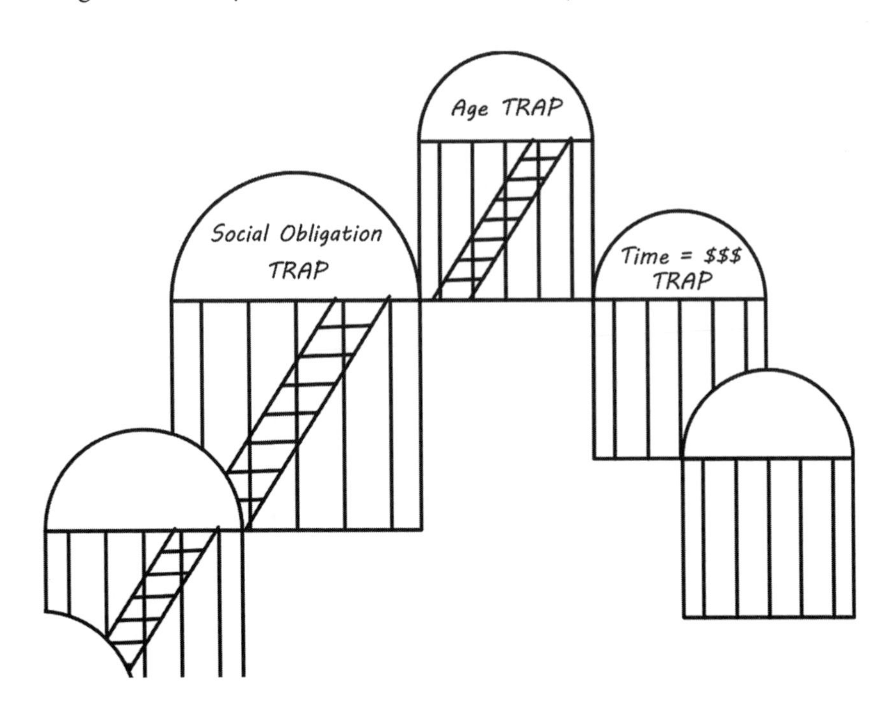

To give a little background, my wife was an all-american volleyball player in college and I didn't suck either. That's a way of saying: "we were pretty good."

I said to her, "Honey, you love art, right?

Reese, "Yes"

Me: "You love soccer too, right?"

Reese: "Yes"

Me: "Great! All the things you love are in your blood. So don't worry about volleyball. You will have fun at whatever you do."

Reese, even at her young age, was feeling the pressure of "the obligation trap." The combination of 1) perfectionism, 2) sequential thinking, and 3) a need for outside validation primes us to live a life that has been mostly chosen for us without us ever knowing.

Add in a fourth element, **being good at something or having legacy status based on what your family was "good" at doing**.

This is when societal obligation kicks in and creates a LOT of pressure to not change course.

If you are good at something (and or you come from a lineage of others that are good at it) *and other people notice and reward you for it,* and that talent, skill, or job can get worked into your conception of who you are, what you do, and even worse what you "should" do. Your ***assigned*** identity. And once that happens, wow, is it hard to break out.

I have made a career of starting businesses then, after a certain number of years, getting bored and transitioning to something new. No one around me has understood why I would leave the success I was in to pursue the unknown next journey. **But sticking with something due to societal obligation is a cancer of the spirit.**

It prevents us from living the lives we were meant to live. Keeps us ignoring that inner voice calling us to go in a direction that is in alignment at a soul level. It is what pushes us into career traps, relationship traps, achievement traps, and—if we aren't paying attention—can push us straight into a life we despise.

As Henry David Thoreau wrote in Walden:

> *"I see young men, whose misfortune it is to have inherited farms, houses, barns, cattle, and farming tools; for these are more* ***easily acquired than got rid of. Why should they begin digging their graves as soon as they are born?***
>
> ***But men labor under a mistake.*** *The better part of the man is soon ploughed into the soil for compost. By necessity, they are employed, laying up treasures which rust will corrupt and thieves break through and steal.* ***It is a fool's life, as they will find when they get to the end of it, if not before."***

This is a perfect depiction of societal obligation and its ultimate outcome. It also lays out the stakes clear as day: if you choose to remain in the trap you will lose the best parts of yourself to it.

Time Collapsers do not confuse their identity with what they do. They do not fear walking away from "success," changing course, or trying something that seems impossible. They don't mind rocking their own boat.

> Challenge Your Assumption: Is the thing you are working on, building, creating, one that has been decided, approved, and/or predetermined by others? If you could start fresh today, without obligation, what would you put your heart into that would create massive value for this life and beyond?

The Time Trap: Time Equals Money

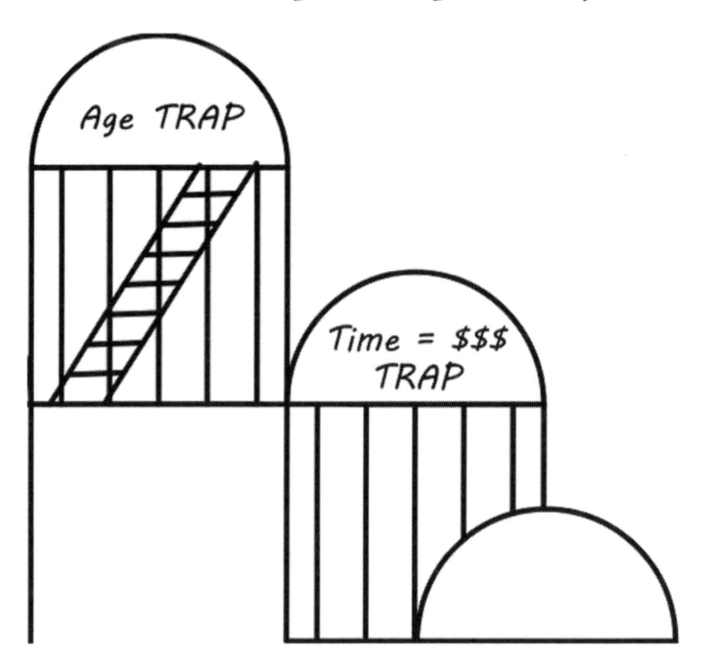

Go to school, get a good job, and you will be financially free—that is so far from the truth. 76% of our population is living paycheck to paycheck. It's even true for high-income earners. The reason for that is a little known Universal Law sets in called: ***Parkinson's Law: Your ability to spend will go up with your ability to earn.***

Debts pile up with mortgage payments, buying a new car, private schools, kids sports, so many things that we won't pass up. We simply defer the payment by accumulating debt. "Oh, it's only 50 grand in debt," we might think, "I can dig my way out of it in the future." When 50 grand becomes 75 grand, we keep going: "I am not going to admit I am in crisis."

The solution society teaches you is: Work for higher wages for longer periods of time. This will NOT be enough to accelerate your income or net worth. What's even more disheartening is the more you make and longer you work, the more the government wants from you in taxes.

In some ways, the "middle ground" becomes a Catch-22. You are working hard, income is going up, you take on more risk, finally turn the corner, and NOW the government wants more. In other words, the more you succeed financially the more you have to give up to time and taxes.

So, how do you escape the time for money trap? You need to understand where leverage occurs in your favor, then spend your time getting there.

Your goal is to create massive financial leverage so you are making money every day whether you are working on that "thing" or not. We will be talking about this in depth later in this book.

The Busy Trap: I'm Successful Because I'm Busy

At a recent meeting I attended, the celebrity speaker (I won't say who) said from stage: "If you just put more time in, you'll increase your chances of success purely because it is mathematical."

I completely disagree.

Somewhere along the way, we've learned to equate an 18-hour workday with being successful. Filling up your calendar, scheduling a ton of meetings, texting all day, and having a ton of clutter around you have somehow come to signal how important you are. But is that actually a real thing? I don't think so.

Most entrepreneurs I see who can't turn the corner have too much shit going on. They are all over the place. They can't think straight. They're teetering on the brink of burning out. What might have made them good has been buried in a sea of B.S.

Time Collapsers focus on the vital few, clear the fluff out of their schedule, and focus their efforts to happen on the MOST IMPORTANT LEVERAGE POINTS to bring them toward their goals.

People are dying to be given permission to STOP doing a bunch of stupid shit and do the one thing they LOVE putting their heart and soul into.

Time Collapsers don't wait.

The "Someday" Trap: Someday I'll Do What I Really Want To Do

There is a false belief, whether conscious or unconsciously decided, that tomorrow will be better or easier or more free than today. It says: "Tomorrow I'll have time."

It's an easy trap to fall into, right? Tomorrow is a blank slate, free of the problems, the distractions, the money pressure, or time pressure you are under today. However, that's just a perception. More problems will be there. More opportunities will be knocking. Here's the truth that Time Collapsers understand:

The ONLY day where you have "power" is today. The only moment you have power is in the moment.

Don't wait to get started.

Don't burn your time and energy on the things that don't directly put you where you want to be. Focus hard and long on the stuff that stirs your soul. Become world-class at it. Share it with the world. Get paid a lot for it—you deserve it.

Don't wait for tomorrow. You future is NOW! The sooner you lock in this understanding, the sooner you can experience full freedom.

Chapter 3:

Losing The Friction

One of the biggest problems with self-help and success systems is that you end up having to do "more" at the end of them than you did when you started. In my experience, when it comes to high-performers and entrepreneurs **"more" can actually start to slow you down!** The way to get back up to speed is by removing what I call "friction" and putting what IS working into alignment.

In other words, the way to create the outcomes you want faster is usually found in knowing or doing less.

I have never seen anyone learn anything faster than my son, Mike, who was 8 at the time, learned lacrosse.

When I sat down to watch his first day at lacrosse camp, I instantly knew Mike was learning from a high level guy. I could tell by the way the coach moved, the way he demonstrated a throw or a catch, and the intensity with which he ran through a simple drill.

Once the coach blew the whistle signaling their first break, I pulled Mike over and said, "Mike, when Coach is talking and demonstrating how to do something here's what I want you to do: block out what he is saying...and just do exactly what he does. Have your body **DO** what he is doing."

Mike nodded, finished his orange slice, took a swig of water and ran back out to the line. As practice picked up again, I could tell my boy had taken what his old man said to heart. The look on his face showed that he was intently *watching* his coach. Rather than following the coach's tips on how to assume a basic defensive stance with his teammates, who were focused solely on keeping their knees bent and body squared, Mike positioned his body to stand just like the pro.

From my sideline view, I could see the difference in Mike's stance: knees bent, *check*; body squared, *check*; chin down, *check;* one foot offset from the other and keeping his weight on the balls of his feet, *check-check*. He moved from side-to-side without ever crossing his feet—even though the coach had not yet made any mention of doing so. He held his stick the way his coach did. In 15 minutes, Mike had gone from looking like the 100% newb that he was to looking like he had months of practice under his belt!

My son is at an age where it's easy and fast to do this **because he has ZERO friction.** He came into his first day of lacrosse camp a completely blank slate—and he was totally okay with it!

We all have this ability to learn at an exponential rate like Mike did, but it's the "being okay with knowing nothing" that we struggle with so much. Why? Because we've been trained to put our filters in place to immediately start comparing brand new information to what we already know as a way of understanding it.

However, if you want to learn something totally new or have a breakthrough that you've never experienced before, trying to match it up to what you already know is actually going to hold you back. ***You must "let go" of what you know in order to allow new model of the world to come into your life.***

If you want to be a Time Collapser, you need to have the ability to learn, assimilate knowledge, **FILTER OUT WHAT DOESN'T BELONG, put into a proper sequence what does, and then get it into your neurology as quickly as humanly possible.**

The first step is to remove the friction. Let's look at a few of the ways that friction builds up and start removing chunks today.

Why Does Friction Build UP?

In my experience, most people who have excessive friction built up share one or more of the following belief systems:

#1: I need to have it all figured out before I get started!

"Once I get to ___________, then I will be ready to write the book."

"After ________, then I will have time to start the business."

"Once the plan is done, we will be ready to launch."

"Once I figure out my life's calling, then I will pour my heart into it!"

There is a false misunderstanding that the people who create "stuff' have it figured out before they launch. The reality is that plans will always change, and the answers are most often found in the process! Your calling can't be found through tests or exams; it's experienced through life.

Don't let the inner voice that tells you need to have a perfect plan mess up what you were put here to do.

Get started! Stop judging yourself!

If you are in the middle of something and having a hard time finishing or taking the next step, APPLY this same principle. Know your benchmarks and keep moving forward.

#2: It's not my fault.

Simple question: Do you approach life with an attitude that everything you have in your life, good, bad, right, wrong, is 1000% your responsibility? If you don't, then you are an easy target for friction and heaviness because the world will find its "victims" and give them more reasons to feel victimized. Remember: Like attracts Like!

If you are serious about being a Time Collapser, then EVERYTHING in your life is your responsibility.

I've had employees sign ridiculously dumb contracts with companies, making poor decisions that cost the company a lot of money. Who do I get upset with? myself...very briefly.

At the end of the day, it's all on me. Life is my greatest teacher and will continue to "teach" me about my journey if I don't "see the lesson." Rather than having to relearn the same painful (and sometimes expensive) lesson, I own up it. And then see how I can learn from it.

Where could I have been smarter?

Where could I have trained them better?

What process could I have had in place to make sure I didn't hire them at all?

Notice how every question places me squarely in the responsibility role?

The more power you give to external decisions or circumstances the more they will slow you down in life, because the friction leaves you feeling helpless. But it's an illusion. As an entrepreneur, after 2008, I saw many successful friends who were in the real estate/mortgage industries get completely crushed. Some bounced back while others have let that experience define their entire lives.

How you define your experiences will either relieve friction from your life or increase it. You always have choice in the matter. You are not a helpless victim. Own your responsibility!

#3: This opportunity may not be the best fit, but it's too good to pass up!

Many of the smartest entrepreneurs I know struggle because of this false belief. They're highly talented and find themselves in "opportunity-seeking land." So they start businesses simply because the opportunity seems great (i.e. Ed, the Dental Marketing Guy).

However, as they soon discover, this path fails to meet expectations—likely because it violates their core values in some way, requires something they don't want to give, or it simply doesn't fit with what they want their life to be. These "opportunity seekers" rarely make it past the first year.

Great things are built by people who have a completely different purpose for continuing to grind through things. It might come out of inspiration or frustration, but they have the passion and persistence to see their vision through. AND THAT VISION MUST BE IN ALIGNMENT WITH THEIR CORE VALUES. Not only that, the process with which they are going after their goals—the work—must also be in alignment in order to have sustained motivation for the final stretch of the journey.

#4: I'll just wait and see.

Sometimes it's not a matter of having the wrong belief system. Sometimes you just have the wrong strategy. And if your strategy is "wait and see," then let me tell you that you're in for a whole lotta friction.

The biggest problem with having the "wrong strategy" is that you end up trying to fix "symptoms" rather than going back to the beginning and readjusting the strategy as a whole. To avoid the friction that comes with spinning your wheels you have to be willing to critically address the What, Why, and How of your strategy. No matter how long you have been working on something, you owe it to yourself to ask the "Zero Based Thinking" question:

- "Knowing what we know now, what would we do differently if we were starting all over again?"
- "Are there any relationships that we wouldn't get into?"
- "Are there any customers that we wouldn't sell to?"
- "Would we be in this business, job, relationship, etc … ?"

Brian Tracy tells us, if your answer to any of this is different than what you are currently doing, then you must ***move swiftly*** to end EVERYTHING you wouldn't be doing.

I've had to swallow that pill many times and simply let months and even years of work get swept under the rug as I shift my focus to a better strategy. I've had to terminate relationships that I knew deep-down were not serving my best interest. I've made the difficult decision to shutter businesses that were "successful," but didn't support where my spirit was asking me to go.

I can honestly tell you, without hesitation, that I never regretted ANY of those decisions I made because of this question.

#5: I'm not in control.

As we learned, your emotional state can exert a lot of control over both your mental and physical states. It can dramatically influence the way you perceive your reality! Your emotional power can be your golden ticket to an abundant life, yes, but the opposite is also true: it can just as easily be your ticket to a life filled with scarcity and problems.

Emotional control is so vital, because not only is it the gateway to how we think, it is the main ingredient for processing external information and events in order to make **meaning** out of it—which can determine how we act. ***Friction builds up when external events are moving you and dictating how you should feel. It will slow you down!*** Stress, anxiety, and fear will slow the speed at which your brain communicates to access information, and that can negatively impact all aspects of your life.

Fortunately, there is a simple way to TAKE BACK CONTROL of your emotional state:

- **Take control of your breath.** Your breath is the power center of everything. It gives you fuel for the mind and the spirit. It can regulate your fight or flight response, and tell you nervous system to get in alignment.
- **Control Your Physiology/Body Posture.** I put a smile on my face for a lot of things. I can tell you with 1000% certainty that putting a smile on your face when stuff really sucks sends a message to your brain to release soothing chemicals that will calm you down.
- **Stand Tall.** Simply by lifting your head and putting your shoulders in a confident posture can put you into a more positive emotional state. The connection between the mind and the body is a powerful thing!
- **Move!** Walk, run, do jumping jacks, or even do something as simple as switching your feet posture. Movement will interrupt any negative flood of emotional response. It can also raise your energy level, which as we know can have a hugely positive effect.
- **Say something positive to yourself or ask an empowering question.** Use these thoughts to open up the control center and empower you.

- "I got this" "I can handle anything that comes my way"
- "Not a problem, easy day"
- What is good about this?
- How do I make something great happen from this?
- This is a blessing in disguise, we just need to find it.
- **See it working out the way you want it to work out.** Ask the question, "What would need to happen in order for this to work out perfectly?" Answer that question with a vivid picture in your mind. The more detail you have, the more your control center knows how to go out and make it happen.
- **Take a positive action to get off at ZERO.** In life, we are polluted with negativity all around us. If you asked the question: "What can I be depressed about today?" the world will serve up plenty of answers for you—but it will get you nowhere. You need to remember, "No amount of feeling bad, will create a result of good." Embrace the idea that your circumstances do not define you.

#6: I signed up for this. I can't quit now.

Nothing great comes from doing things out of obligation. If you stopped and examined many of the things that cause friction in your life, you would likely see a pattern of obligation. Doing things for others because you feel you must, rather than wanting to do so. Attending "networking" events, because you think that is what you have to do. Saying "yes" to projects because you don't want to disappoint someone else. It's all one big, friction-loaded trap.

Recognizing this, then freeing yourself from anything that doesn't have alignment with your purpose and intention in life will get rid of that friction. ***A simple test is to ask yourself: "Does this decision feel heavy or light?"*** If it's heavy, then most of the time it's the wrong thing to do, or the wrong path to go down.

#7: I can't just quit a friendship/partnership/relationship.

A great relationship will allow you to soar, while the wrong one(s) will tear you down. To use a simple term: "iron sharpens iron." ***If you surround yourself with people who make you better and allow you to be yourself, then you will grow. If you surround yourself with people who stifle your vision, judge you for who you are, or expect you to stay at status quo, then you will continue to be stuck.***

When you start down the path towards fulfilling your vision, you will encounter a large number of people who have known the "old" you and unconsciously want to keep you there. They aren't doing it to hurt you, they just want to keep their model of the world intact.

You MUST be okay with simply choosing a new path that leads you towards new and empowering relationships. To do otherwise is a low-energy move and nothing good will come out of it. Simply notice when a relationship is no longer nurturing, supportive, or synergistic and make decisions that put you in a more abundant context, environment, or path.

So don't hold on to the relationships that aren't serving you or sharpening you.

#8: Judgement

"When you judge another, you don't define them. You define Yourself!" Wayne Dyer has said, and I couldn't agree more.

When we filter information, we unconsciously ask the question: "What does this mean?"

In some ways, we are always judging information that comes in. Interpreting the meaning is natural, but being attached to a conclusion that you make is where friction occurs. Does this conclusion support you? Does it allow you to have flexibility in your decision making, or does it cause rigidity?

If it doesn't provide more clarity and flexibility, then you need to dump it. This is a strategy I've implemented in my own life. Rather than judge someone or something (and, in doing so, letting it define me) I imagine having 4 quadrants in my life, and I have deemed one of them the "box."

If a judging thought does not support me. I put it in that box and have no feelings towards it. I completely disassociate from it. That's just my process. You may find one that serves you better, but the point is to not allow your judgements to have undue influence over your thoughts and actions.

#9: Phew! I'm so overwhelmed. It's great!

Our society has made it a badge of courage the more overwhelmed you are. The busier you are the more successful you must be, right? WRONG! This idea that you have to constantly be doing more will only weigh you down with MORE FRICTION.

I've had employees and entrepreneurs who were extremely valuable, but then became less and less effective as they took on more and more work. They failed to realize that ***the true measure of value is the effectiveness of the effort...not quantity of effort*** and they paid the price.

The secret to overcoming overwhelm is:

- Understand and regularly return to your "why."
- Have a clear picture of where you want to be in 1- 3 years.
- Internalize what's really important. Once you have priorities clear...it's easy to say "NO."
- Dump all low energy relationships, customers, and activities that suck up your energy. Remember, it's about doing LESS!

- Apply your energy where it will count the most. We will be discussing the Pareto (or "80/20") Principle in depth later on, but the key takeaway now is that you're better off applying to resources to the areas that will deliver the biggest return.

#10: I need approval and permission from others

The last friction point I want to address in this chapter is our desire for others' approval.

The biggest thing that you need to realize right now is that NO ONE can see the world through your lenses. Only you can hear the Whisper of your soul and march to that drummer. If you want to "take the road less traveled" to quote Scott M. Peck, you need to realize that it's a "less" traveled road. Therefore, you will find very few people who get what you are trying to do.

When I reflect on every pivotal point of my life that took me far, there was always very little understanding from those around me. They literally couldn't see my vision...even if I spoke about it for hours. It wasn't their fault. It's just not possible.

If I had sat and waiting for their permission, or for them to finally "get it" I wouldn't have accomplished half of the things I've done in my life. You must ***initiate*** the movement under the water, be the blower of the wind and the force behind the power. Once you understand this and you begin to follow your own inner voice you will be set free.

Of course there will be times where you desire to get approval and/or advice from those you admire. Just make sure they are A) qualified to give you feedback, input, and coaching; and b) remember that, at the end of the day, they can only offer their perception. You don't have to listen.

WHAT WILL YOU ACCOMPLISH WHEN YOU ARE FREE FROM FRICTION?

There is a new breed entrepreneurs that is ever-increasing, with very little friction, who are creating the future. Many people have made millions replicating what is already there.

Time Collapsers may take concepts that already exist and make them better, thus creating something that has never existed before. Their souls are alive. Their passion is alive. They have broken free from the friction and are literally changing the world.

In the next section, we will explore how much is actually possible when you create this freedom for yourself. The results will amaze you.

Chapter 4:

The Freedom Question

As I mentioned in the last chapter, high performers don't look for more stuff to do, they seek out more distinctions.

One key thing that holds us back from achieving our next breakthrough is our perception of our current situation. The reason being that where we currently are is where we hold all of our problems, whether real or perceived. Our limiting constraints. Existing relationships. Financial status and limitations. They're all hanging out in our present reality.

While studying high performers, I've found there is a distinct pattern of mental breakthrough, that I'll call "The Freedom Question!"

It's a process similar to time travel, where you leave the present moment mentally and shoot out into the future, BEYOND any problem or limitation, and then ask a simple question:

"Wouldn't it be great if... (INSERT YOUR IDEAL SITUATION)?"

Whether you come to this question out of frustration, inspiration, anger, loss, hope, happiness, a desire to take a stand or prove others wrong, or a combination of many things, there is a point where these emotions ***get flipped*** into a very resourceful, very powerful future-focused question that begins the process of creation.

This question is powerful because it creates freedom from ALL limitations.

WHY THIS QUESTION WORKS

We all see things we would like to change in our current life. It's very easy to get stuck on "what is" and fail to transition into what is possible. "Wouldn't it be great if…" creates a chain of thoughts that take you out of the present moment and moves you forward, all the way past the problem ALREADY being solved.

After all, where are all solutions hiding? **Beyond the obstacle!**

Thinking past the obstacle is a tool to transition a problem into something really productive. Most high-level thinkers or creators have an ability for seeing what is not already there. "Wouldn't it be great if…" creates the free space necessary to do so.

Let's take a look at couple cases in which this Freedom Question has created some awesome impact.

Wouldn't it be great if we could grow crops without needing acres of land?

Vertical Farming….

Wouldn't it be great if we could buy cool glasses without forking over a ton of cash?

Glasses are expensive. Neil Blumenthal and his friends, David Gilboa, Andrew Hunt, and Jeffrey Raider wondered: "Do they have to be?" The four guys, all MBA students at the time, had studied the success stories behind Amazon and Zappos; they knew people were becoming more and more open to buying just about everything online. If people are comfortable buying a pair of shoes without trying them on, they figured, they might be open to doing the same with eyewear.

ESPECIALLY if it meant they could save a bunch of money.

Nicknamed "the Netflix of eyewear"[2] Warby Parker is now considered a "unicorn" of startup success. Free from the burden of high overhead costs like rent (until recently, the company only operated online) and licensing fees (they design their own frames, rather than pay for a luxe name), the company sells their frames for around $100. Sales took off quickly and haven't slowed down since. Warby Parker recently received a $1.2 BILLION valuation!

Wouldn't it be great if we could buy what we needed without going to the store and get same day or next day delivery?

Amazon.com is such a prolific entity at this point that it's easy to forget that they used to sell only books. As the internet revolution exploded, Jeff Bezos decided to start an online business.

Wouldn't it be great if we could send and receive money while also protecting our bank information?

Paypal

The good news is that you can model these "thinking" processes.

What follows are some exercises you can walk through to practice the Freedom Question in your own life. I'll follow along, outlining some examples of what mine might be now or have in the past so so you can get a feel for what I'm talking about.

I suggest that you set a timer for at least 10 minutes to allow you to have time to "think" and process.

Feel free to pour yourself a cup of coffee (or a glass of wine) and get comfortable. Turn off your inner critic. And remember: you have no limits. Anything is possible!

---

[2] Wong, Danny (November 29, 2010), "GQ Calls it the Netflix of Eyewear", *The Huffington Post*

Exercise #1 — Literally See Beyond the Obstacle:

Here's a sample of what mine might be:

Wouldn't it be great if my business, job, profession, career...

- **Was a cash machine,** throwing off $100,000 to (INSERT NUMBER) of net profit every month.
- **Had an outstanding team** of highly motivated and smart people who loved coming to work every day and felt passionate about driving the business forward.
- **Allowed me to work solely on my strengths** so that I felt rejuvenated, happy, and inspired transforming lives every day.
- **Donated** $250,000 to charity.

Fill in the blanks:

If I was sitting here in one year, wouldn't it be great if my business....

- ______________________________
- ______________________________
- ______________________________
- ______________________________

The great thing about the Freedom Question is that you can apply it to any area of your life. You can do this with your spouse regarding your family, the goals you have for you kids.

If you aren't married, then you can do this for the perfect partner you'd like to create in your life. Want better health? Awesome! Do this exercise!

The goal is to move your thinking beyond your perceived limitations so you experience thinking from this new place of possibility.

Exercise #2 — Bring it into Your Present:

After you go through the first part of the exercise, now it's time to put yourself in the future with these goals already realized.

Here's my example:

***Isn't it great that* the business...**

- **Is transforming the lives of thousands of people with autoimmune disease.**
- **Raising awareness and improving care across the globe.**
- **Paying us $200,000 and month.**
- **Inspiring Millions of people yearly**
- **It allows us to have maximum flexibility, time freedom, and freedom**

Finish this statement:

Isn't it great that...

- ______________________________
- ______________________________
- ______________________________
- ______________________________

The idea here is to bring your goal into your present thinking **as though it is already a reality.** What does it look like? What are you doing? What is the impact or contribution you are making? Write all of this down and try to really see it!

Exercise #3: Look Back at How You Did It:

Have you ever noticed that if you look back on a goal you achieved, problem you faced, or challenge that you ALREADY solved a long time ago it doesn't feel like it was that hard to do?

There is something magical that happens in our mind when we move an event further into our past. It's as though our mind reorganizes our relationship with it, giving us new insights that weren't there before. I'd be willing to bet that if you did the first two exercises you are already experiencing some of that. So, this simple exercise is another way of supercharging what you have already done.

In this exercise, I want you go out another 3-5 years past the accomplishment of your goal and have conversation with a reporter from a famous magazine or television show about "Why?" And "How?" you made it happen.

I always use Oprah or Ellen Degeneres. Funny right? Anyhow, you can use whomever you enjoy listening to. Have fun with this!

- What was your first step?
- What made you decide to get started on this path?
- What was unique about your journey?
- Why would others tell your story?
- Who was involved?
- Who were your biggest supporters?
- Who were your mentors and your models?
- Who was no longer supportive, and how did you replace those relationships in your life?
- What problems did you overcome?
- What books did you read? What seminars did you attend?

Take 10-15 minutes to daydream and write out your interview. By the end of the exercise, you will have the bones of a plan to at least get started toward overcoming the obstacles you fear stand in your way. The Freedom Question will have expanded your idea of what's possible.

You can make this easy and fun too! One little trick I use is the process of walking and talking—it works like magic for me. If at any time this exercise feels heavy or hard, simply go for a walk and talk through these exercises in your mind. You'll find the energy lift makes it a lot easier!

And, as final bit of advice, find someone with whom you can share your responses. At our seminars, we keep it really easy and light. Usually people get into groups of 2 or 3 and share their answers. The act of speaking out loud adds a ton of crystal clarity, opportunity for more insights, and also puts your ideal future out there to begin to manifest.

Attend Time Collapsing Mega-Conference LIVE!
"Real World, Multi-Million Dollar to Billion Dollar Entrepreneurs Share Their No-Holds Barred Approach For Hyper-Growth, Leaping To The Top, And Time Collapsing!"

Each year, we assemble an elite group of high performing entrepreneurs to share their "Time Collapsing" secrets for rapid success. You will learn advanced strategies that can only be taught by those who have been, in-the-trenches.

Whether you are starting, in a growth phase, or hitting a ceiling and looking for the slight edge, there will be something for you!

www.TimeCollapsingMegaconference.com

Time Collapsing Academy & Mastermind!
Get Personally Trained By Ed O'Keefe & An Elite Cadre of World Class Entrepreneurs!

You can get access to the highest level of real-world marketing, advertising, traffic, and sales processes with Time Collapsing Academy. An elite training program for entrepreneurs who are looking for rapid growth, more FREE Time, and truly wealthy life.

Time Collapsing Academy is the by-product of over 17 years of entrepreneurship experience, modeling best practices, and discovering the best way to accelerate all types of business models!

Find out what level of training is best suited for you at:

www.TimeCollapsingAcademy.com

Subscribe and Listen To Ed O'Keefe Show Podcast on Itunes!

Ed interview experts like: Jesse Itzler, Author of Living With A Seal! Jeff Usner: 50,000 Leads A Day Who Builds Houses and Schools For Orphans. Lewis Howes- Author of School of Greatness! Roland Frasier- Behind the Scenes Of Triple Digit Growth 3 Years In A Row! Com Mirza- Hear How Com sold his company for just under $500,000,000 after almost losing everything.

Plus, you can listen and watch Ed's Solo-Episodes Called The Time Collapsing Files!!!

www.EdOKeefeshow.com

PART II

Chapter 5:

The Tectonic Shift, Tsunami, and Undertow: Understanding The Power of Directional Pull

Mark Twain said, "The two most important days in your life are when you are born and when you find out WHY!"

That's great Mark!

Two key days—and one of them, I peed all over myself and don't remember a single bit.

So, that leaves one more day to look forward to...and there's a strong chance I won't really know "WHY" until after I'm gone.

Twain's quote sounds nice and all, but it's pretty worthless as far as I'm concerned. Worse than that, it demonstrates the exact kind of thinking that I believe slows so many of us down.

I don't know about you, but the whole "Find Your Purpose™" thing is a hard conversation for me to have. It's not that I think finding a mission or passion that really drives you is a bad thing—that couldn't be further from how I feel.

What concerns me is the idea that you need to have it all figured out before you get started. Think about it: if you sit and do nothing until you have crystal-clear clarity on your purpose, then your "purpose" is actually getting in your way!

I believe the stronger choice is to **get moving!** Which brings us to: The Tectonic Shift, Tsunami, and Undertow...the elements that create Directional Pull, one of the key elements of the Time Collapsing system.

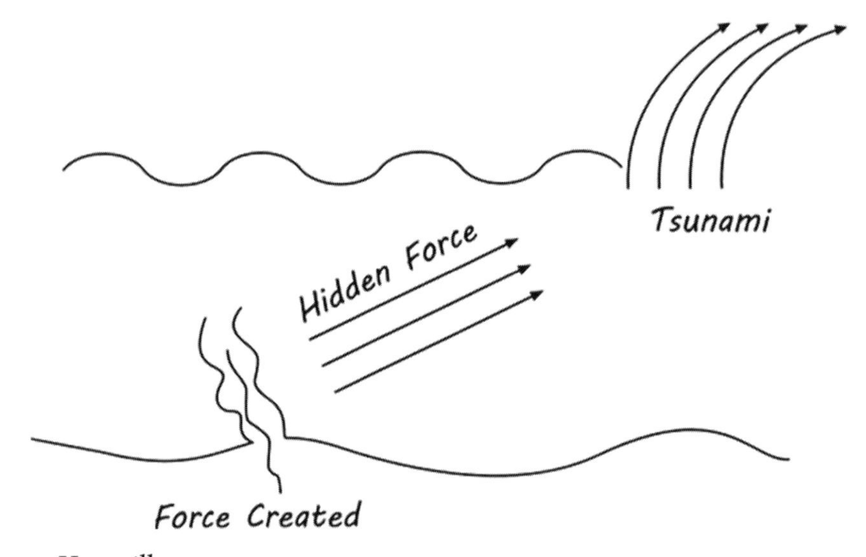

You will:

A: find your passion, purpose, and mission

B: have a lot of fun, experience success, as you confusedly stumble forward in this world trying to find your purpose. You may find that *THAT* is your purpose after all!

The Dirtiest Man On TV Takes OFF!

A great example of directional pull is the famous voice and recognizable wit of Mike Rowe, currently working as the narrative voice on the hit TV show Deadliest Catch. Mike has become famous for his shows "Dirty Jobs" and "Someone's Gotta do it!"

He's doing what he wants to do, but would also tell you that it's a big mistake to "follow your passion"; instead "chase opportunity," and then backfill the passion when you find the right opportunity.

What attracted me to share his story was that Mike bounced around finding his direction and spent years as a QVC pitchman, honing his skills and becoming an artful communicator and salesperson. The toughest job ever is getting people to move their butts off a couch and pick up the phone to buy something.

This, my friends, is probably one of the hardest things to do. Getting measured literally every 30-60 minutes to see how you are doing, because the sales coming through the phones directly correlate to HOW GOOD YOU ARE and whether you get to keep your job. You'd have to be desperate, broke, or an aspiring to take that gig. To make it worse, he worked the 12:00am–6:00am graveyard shift.

Finally, after making fun of products and "belittling callers"[3] one time too many, Mike was fired. Then, through a horrible miscalculation, he pitched a three-hour special to the Discovery Channel that featured him getting down and dirty in some of the filthier professions and industries around the country. You guessed it: "Dirty Jobs." The network scooped it up and Mike found himself the host of his own show.

His career took off and over the next decade he became known to the world as "the dirtiest man on TV." But when he decided he was ready for a change, he wasn't sure how to make it happen. Where could TV's dirtiest man go next?

The answer, it would turn out, was *everywhere.* Mike became a voi-

---

[3] "Exclusive: Mike Rowe Talks "Human Planet"" Mental Floss. April 08, 2011. Accessed June 28, 2016. http://mentalfloss.com/article/27466/exclusive-mike-rowe-talks-human-planet.

ceover actor, and has narrated hundreds of documentaries and been the voice (and sometimes the face) of commercial brands, including Ford. Then came the opportunity to make another show, called, "Somebody's Gotta Do It" for CNN.

Mike Rowe didn't predetermine that his mission was to be a voiceover actor or to have a top-rated show on the Discovery Channel. He bounced around until the right thing stuck...and off it went. By continuing to move in the directions he felt pulled toward, Mike was creating a Tectonic Shift, his time on QVC and his voiceover work, for years before his Tsunami of Success came in. It was his LACK OF CLARITY that lead to his success.

But here's the funny thing about your "Tectonic Shift"...

Your results might not be noticed during this phase. The same way a tsunami, which is caused by a tectonic shift hundreds of miles offshore, can only be detected by radar until it its momentum begins to build a wave. The tsunami wave shows up "unexpectedly," leaving those on the beach wondering where it came from.

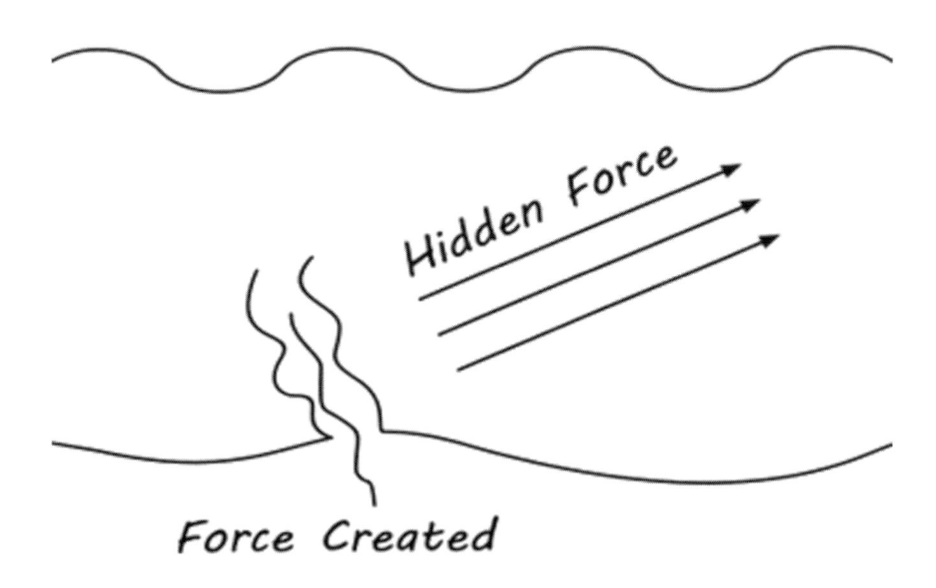

And if we're thinking about this tsunami as a metaphor for success, that "unexpected" wave is what everyone else would call "an overnight success." When your Tsunami of Success rolls in, people are likely to comment about how you came out of nowhere, but you will say to yourself:

"I've been grinding away at this my entire life."

You can see the invisible dots in your past that have brought you to this point. That IS your personal tectonic shift whether you know it or not.

As you read these words, right now, you ***ALREADY*** have momentum ... even if it doesn't feel that way. What do you think would happen if you were to bring that momentum to a full stop while you figure out a place to direct it?

Therefore, by trying to know with such specificity and crystal clarity what your success will look like, you might have put yourself in a TRAP, slowing your momentum and stressing you out. Instead of focusing on your PURPOSE, put your focus on your DIRECTION.

This leads us to the principle of **the Trim Tab Theory of Success.**

In his book, *Mastery – A Technology of Excellence and Personal Evolution,* author Tim Piering shares the concept of the Trim Tab Theory. It states that if two ships were going to leave port on the east coast of United States and you simply change the trim tab, a tiny mechanism on the rudder, of one of the ships by 3%, you would notice no significant difference in the ship's direction for many, many miles.

But by the time the ships reached their destination in Europe, they would be hundreds of miles apart.

So how does the Trim Tab Theory apply to us?

I bring it up to show the difference between setting a direction and setting a GOAL. If the ship's goal was to arrive in Spain and, thanks to a wonky trim tab, it landed in Portugal then the trip would be considered a failure.

If the ship's captain opts for a *direction*—Europe—instead of a goal, then as long as they find land they have succeeded. If they set course for Spain and have to change course because of weather, that's okay.

Most people fail at "success principles" because they don't know how to handle the reality of the path. As I audited my own goal setting routine, I noticed that many of the goals I set didn't hit their target. Had I remained unaware, I would likely have followed every step I had laid out and felt very confused when, years later, I realized I had ended up in the wrong place.

"Goals" are vital, because they give us directional anchor points to target and move toward. But they aren't everything.

Time Collapsers either consciously or unconsciously realize that the goals are all about directional pull...and it's the process of moving towards those goals that can prove really valuable. They don't worry about how they get there as long as they get the end result they want.

Ideally you'll become obsessed with mastering the process of goal achievement, but not attached to the end-result, because the journey will forge you, enlighten you, and give you insights that change your "outcome goal." You'll understand that what you thought was important BEFORE your started...might not seem as essential later on.

The reality is: Goals change. Priorities change. Circumstances change. Talent is not created equally, and sometimes things just don't work out... and sometimes they do.

Which means if you know which areas of your life you want to focus on: Financially, emotionally, mentally, and have loving relationships, then:

a. You set out in a direction that ONLY sets the odds in your favor,
b. Then you are creating a directional pull that helps you accomplish a ton of things...many of which may be unexpected. Stay flexible!

c. Understand that everything that shows up is there to guide you in it's own way.

d. Apply "never giving up" to this ***process*** NOT an outcome goal... and you're as guaranteed to find success, adventure, and a life that lights you up.

The funny thing is, in doing so, you might end up finding your purpose. In my experience, **"purpose" is found IN THE PROCESS!**

You can take on small challenges or ENORMOUS challenges, but most importantly get dialed into the *process* of making them happen...and loosen up your attachment to a specific outcome.

Here are some examples of goals written in typical, well-formed, structure:

My goal is to earn $500,000 this year.

I happily will lose 25 lbs by December 31st.

Now, if you say to yourself:

"Okay, I'm going to focus on creating the ideal situation that I "intend" to occur. I'm going to get clear on what I can control, influence, and generate. I KNOW with certainty that if I do these things...I will output a better self whether I win, lose, succeed, or fail."

"How do I create a context in which my goal is 100% certain to occur?"

"Who is the mentor(s) that I can hire/learn from/ follow who have the path n plan?"

"Who has already done this?"

When you take this approach you can generate a powerful "tectonic shift" of incredible momentum. Obstacles will arrive, but they will also be in the company of solutions. As your SPEED and your momentum build, you'll notice that "perfect coincidences" start happening. The right person, idea, funding, or a multitude of other things start working for you.

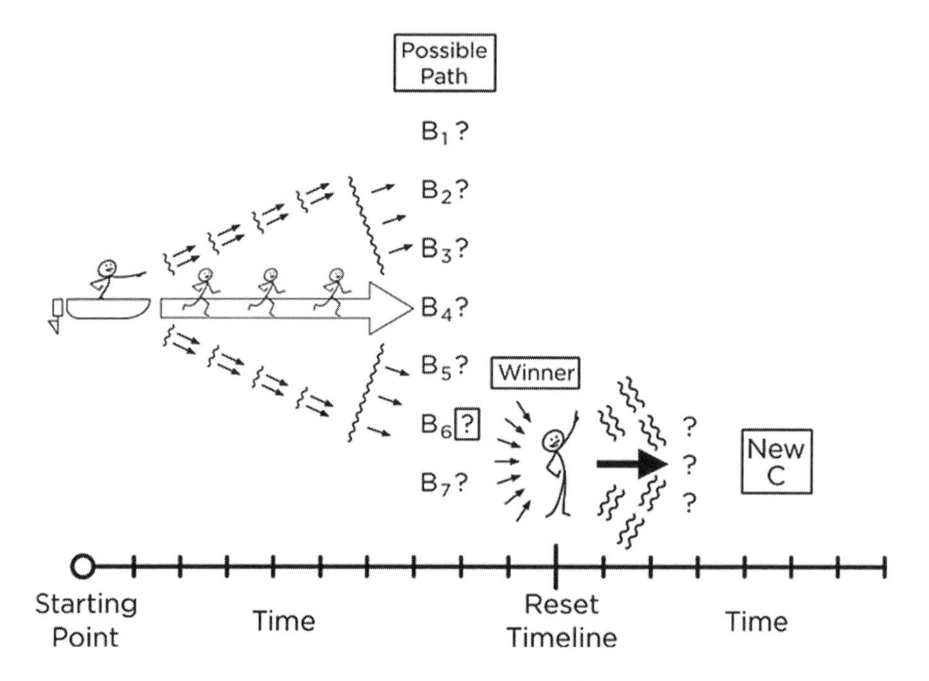

Small victories that are hit consistently even in the face of micro-failures set you up to win in the long run due to Power Laws. When you have micro- wins, it's easier to experience confidence, gratitude, and momentum.

Focus on the small wins, learn from the small fails, and you'll learn a pattern of positive reinforcement that subconsciously creates a powerful PULL. **You are NOT waiting til you hit your goal to experience happiness and excitement.**

Be Aware of The Undertow

There is a paradox to success that you must be aware of though. At the same time your Tsunami of Success is finally hitting, after you've been grinding all these years, there is an undertow that is being generated too.

What does the Undertow do? It pulls you back down!

Who gets killed during an undertow of a real-life tsunami? Those not aware of it. Similarly, those who are not aware of the Undertow that accompanies a Tsunami of Success can be pulled under.

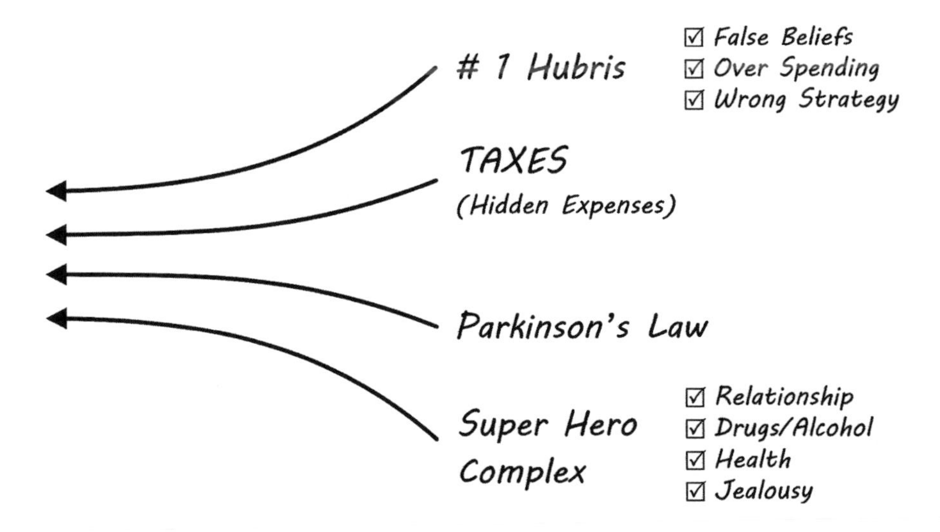

Artists, Athletes, Celebrities, and entrepreneurs fall prey to this. When "success" comes riding in, everyone around wants to tell them how great they are. It's a TRAP.

In James C. Collins's book, *Why the Mighty Fall: And Why Some Companies Never Give In,* he offers an in-depth look at why large companies fail. He cites hubris as the Number One cause. Arrogance, cockiness, and a false belief that a good thing is going to last forever.

Remember, you are always creating the next tsunami in your life and constantly making trim tab decisions. **Your aim should be to consistently come from the same place and ride one wave to the next while being aware of the Undertow.**

One of the best secrets I use for avoiding the undertow is to keep the circle of people around me to those who are looking out for my best interest and are not afraid to tell me when they think I'm "off."

Applying This Chapter:

Here are three "mind-freeing" questions that I'd like you to go through to identify any potential obstacles that are blocking your momentum right now, so you can then set them aside.

Grab a piece of paper and pen to start brainstorming.

Question #1: If you had $10,000,000 (or more) in the bank right now and never had to work another day in your life, what would you spend your time doing?

Question #2: If you had a magic wand, and all obstacles that you perceive right now, were solved and behind you now, what would your future look like moving forward?

Question #3: If you had to actually pay $50,000 a year to be allowed to do something...what would that activity, role, career, or contribution be?

Read through your answers to see if you can identify the problems those hypothetical scenarios solve. Those are likely your momentum blockers.

Pivotal Trim Tab Decisions:

Am I open to the possibility that my future may combine elements of what has already been done, knowing that I could use the existing example to reverse engineer my path?

Am I open to reevaluating how my business is structured? Am I willing to change how I am accustomed to operating so that I can free up time, space, and creative energy?

What type of business am I going to start?

- a cash flow business,
- a lifestyle business,
- or a business to grow and sell for a major payout?

What are the top one or two skill sets that I personally want to develop over the next 3 to 5 years that I will enjoy mastering and would make the biggest difference towards my overall direction?

Which direction or opportunity am I going to concentrate my focus? (Limitless possibilities is a guaranteed way to get destroyed.)

Do I have one thing that is currently working? Or am I burning my energy on loose threads and dead-end directions?

How am I going to measure my life net worth? What does success look like?

How do I want to feel on a daily basis emotionally as that will affect my directional pull and undertow?

How can I frame my life in a way that makes it easy and seemingly effortless?

I can't stress enough to you how POWERFUL it is to be aware of your momentum and the things that might be slowing it down. Choose your direction, feel your tectonic shift kick in, see your wins and losses as spurring you you on, and get ready for your Tsunami of Success!

Chapter 6:

FILTERS OF GREATNESS

"I heard you guys were awesome tonight!" my bartender said to me. She was referring to our Volleyball team. We had all bellied up to the bar at our local drinking hole, Mr. Bee's in Davenport Iowa, after our afternoon match against Division I powerhouse, Lewis University. Now it was almost 1:30 am.

"Yeah, it was awesome!" I replied.

What was funny about this is we probably lost 0-3, or possibly won one game in the 3-out-of-5 match. However, you would have never known this if you were with us at the bar.

After we got a few drinks in us, the only thing that was coming out of our mouths were the plays that we won. The amazing block, dig, or kill that we could remember. At this point, any mistakes we made were completely deleted. After all, why share our volleyball setbacks with the people at the bar?

If you were to listen to any one of us, you would think we dominated the match and were well on our way to winning a National Title.

This my friends is what I call: "The Art of Reality Bending!"

Despite the alcohol and our crazy imagination, we ALL dramatically changed our reality based on our "filters." What we allow in, what we delete out, and what we choose to make things MEAN.

To understand how this happens, look at how actors take on roles. One of the best is WIll Smith. In an interview, Will shared how he resonated with Chris Gardner so much his reality changed to to meet elements of Gardner's world:

> "Chris and I were raised in **very spiritual households**, and **believed wholeheartedly that our thoughts, our feelings, our dreams, our ideas are physical in the universe.**
>
> That if we dream something, if we picture something -- we commit ourselves to it -- that has a physical thrust towards realization that we can put into the universe."

If Will is right, and our thoughts, feelings, and dreams are PHYSICAL elements in the universe, then by goodness, what will you make *your reality* out to be?

Obviously, everyone has a unique answer to this question. BUT, no matter how different the responses may be, I'm willing to bet everyone is starting from the exact same place: the reality they already know. That mindset can only get you so far.

It reminds me of a great quote by Marshall Goldsmith, who says: "The same thinking that got you here will not get you there!" In other words, the thinking and action that has brought you to exactly where you're sitting now cannot be used to take yourself in a new direction. **If you want to create a new reality, you need to use different tools.**

If this is true, then we need new thinking. *Hmmm.* But what does that really mean?

We've got to expand our list of what's possible to include things that don't exist yet.

I'd like to share with you that this is possible. The problem, to this point, is that you've only been taught how to see the world through one lense with limited capabilities.

Before we get to how you can create a new reality, we've got to do a little bit of groundwork to further understand how our reality is formed. Don't worry, it's simple and easy. This won't hurt a bit.

THE FILTERS THAT CREATE OUR REALITY (OR THE FILTERS OF GREATNESS)

Every second, millions of bits of information are being processed by our eyes, then being filtered and communicated to our brain. That's WAY more than we're capable of managing. According to a MIT Study, the human mind can only consciously process 60 bits of information per second.

Since there is too much information coming into our heads to process all of it, our brains generalize, delete, and prioritize what's important. That's where our filters come in, and that's how our perception of reality gets defined (and distorted).

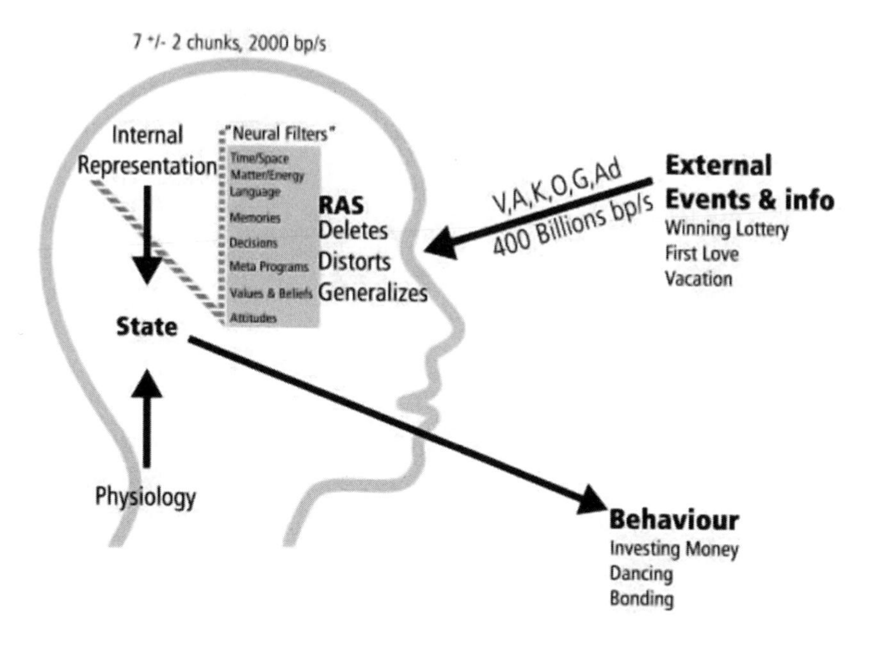

Instead of seeing the world around you as it really is, you create a MAP of reality—but no matter how good you are, your map can't ever be REAL. As AlfredKorzybski said: " **The map is not the territory.**" It metaphorically illustrates the differences between belief and reality. Map lines don't actually exist on the earth itself.

This means our perception of the world is being generated by our brain and can be considered as a 'map' of reality written in neural patterns. Reality exists outside our mind but we can construct models of this 'territory' based on what we glimpse through our senses. And those models are completely malleable.

This brings us to the COOLEST PART! Imagine if everything that came your way was processed in such a way that it served you rather than working against you? It's within your reach. By understanding how to utilize filters you can do what so many Time Collapsers have implemented in their lives: bend reality to what you want it to be.

So, let's take a look at how we form our perception. What filters the information that comes in and contributes to your "REALITY"?

#1: IDENTITY: HOW DO YOU SEE YOURSELF IN THIS WORLD?

How do you view yourself? Who are you? How do you fit into your society? No matter how you answer those questions, your brain is going to find information and feedback that reinforces your belief.

Your identity is a POWERFUL filter. It directly affects what you feel is important, the things you think you're capable of doing, how you talk to yourself, how you expect yourself to respond in certain situations, what you think is vital to study, and the list goes on and on.

Out of all the potential areas to make a change, adopting a more empowering self-image or self-identification has the most profound and long lasting impact.

> Create a Time Collapsing Filter: Stop thinking about what you need to do to achieve the outcome you want. Instead, place your focus on who you need to *be*. Ask yourself: ***"Who must I become in order to make all these goals (and more) happen naturally in my life?"***
>
> Where would you like to see the biggest shift in your life? Imagine that area of your life is flowing more perfectly than you could ever imagine, who would you have to be in order to allow and create that type of life?

#2: VALUE SYSTEM: WHAT MATTERS THE MOST TO YOU?

Your value system is the core way of prioritizing and appointing value in your life. The things that you value highly will inform your filters. By answering the question "What is important to you?" and then laying out those things in sequence of priority, you can find out almost everything you need to know about your value system.

Create a Time Collapsing Filter: It's essential that you determine whether there are any gaps between what you think you value and what you actually value (think of it also as the gap between what you *say* you like to do and what you actually *choose* to do). One point of friction that prevents people from Time Collapsing is the lack of alignment between their perceived and actual values.

It takes experience to know the difference, but it helps to at least put some awareness of what your core values are. Then ask yourself: ***"Is my work consistent with my core values?"***

Lay out what you hope to accomplish by your endeavor. The more specific you are the better. Lay out the answers to what is important to you and how will you know when you are accomplishing it. Then put those in sequence so you can see if there's any mismatch or incongruence.

#3: BELIEF SYSTEMS: WHAT DO YOU BELIEVE IS REAL?

Belief systems are the stories we tell ourselves to define our personal sense of "reality." Every human being has a belief system that they utilize, and it is through this mechanism that we individually "make sense" of the world around us.

It has been said that a person will do anything to support what they believe is real, even if it's the most destructive thing for them. We all know people who seem to find no shortage of evidence that their life sucks, why they suck, and why everyone around them sucks. Needless to say, you can predict what behavior, attitude, and life that person will have. However the good news is that "beliefs" are flexible and can be changed to support us any way that we want them to.

> Create a Time Collapsing Filter: Time Collapsers reset their beliefs of what is possible to get their mind and body into a place that allows them to push through to where they want to be. One thing they understand is that beliefs are fluid and changeable. Case in point: there was a time in your life when you believed a rabbit ran around your backyard and hid eggs there, or that a tooth-obsessed fairy put money under your pillow when you slept. Whether the story was real or not, it influenced your behavior—but I doubt that it would now. Ask yourself: ***"In what other ways has my belief system changed before?"***
>
> The coolest thing is that by identifying and adopting belief systems of others you can then "install" them into your filters. Over time, you start "seeing" the world through their eyes. Can you think of someone (or multiple people) who have the achieved the level of success you want for yourself? How do they see the world? What sort of belief systems do they adhere to?

#4: Emotional states: How do you feel?

One of the key things I learned when training in NLP and hypnosis is that your brain drives your emotional state; in turn, your emotional state can influence how your brain processes your reality. In other words, the stories bouncing around between your ears have the power to affect your actual physical reality for better or worse.

Create a Time Collapsing Filter: Ask yourself: ***"What are the most common emotional states, both empowering and disempowering, that I experience on a daily basis?"***

There are a number of ways you can alter your emotional state (and your reality) to serve you better. Let's take a look at some of them.

THOUGHTS OF POWER: Researchers say that we have 50 to 60 thousand thoughts a day. 90% of them are from the day before, and the day before that, and the day before that; and most are negative or disempowering. If this is true then one of the first things you need to do in order to control your filters is to rewire and retrain your brain to stay positive empowering things.

Get up and get moving. Jump around, do some push-ups, or go run around the block. Bring your body's energy up and tell yourself one of the following phrases five times:

I got this! We can do this all day!

I'm a warrior! I am powerful!

I am strong! I believe in myself!

I can handle anything that comes my way!

THOUGHTS OF SELF-COMPASSION: High-performers tend to be harder on themselves then they need to be. When it comes to assessing your work, your skills, or even your capabilities, I'm sure no one is tougher on you than you are on yourself. When your self-critical thoughts start running amok (hey, it happens), it can be entirely too easy to stand in your own way.

Time Collapsers understand that each of us is in control of our own thoughts, and they have the tools to gain control and redirect the thoughts that will work against them. The key word is "redirect" because I can guarantee with 100% certainty you will you will stay stupid stuff to yourself in the future.

When you hear yourself say something that's disempowering or unresourceful simply say to yourself "Ed, that's ridiculous...the reality is (insert something more empowering)." If you find yourself saying any of these things: "I'm fat, ugly, stupid, unqualified, too young, too old, too inexperienced, not tech savvy enough," it's safe to say that your thoughts are working against you. Here's how you can hit the "reset button" and get yourself back on track.

> Say to yourself, "Cancel. Cancel. That's Ridiculous!" Then say something that is way more empowered to direct your thought process to where you want to go.

So let's say you catch yourself saying something like, "I'm too fat and always fall off my diet!" Stop that line of thinking in its tracks by saying, "Cancel. That's ridiculous. My body is getting into better shape every day and I feel great. This setback has just created more clues on how I will succeed in the future."

There are more strategies, obviously, to gain control of your thoughts, but a couple quick ones are:

Get Kinesthetic: Have you ever noticed that negative voices are loudest when you are sedentary or inactive? Do the opposite! Taking action and getting your body physically moving will shut down most of your chatter mind. Even something as simple as putting a smile on your face and shaking your hands out can radically change how you feel.

This is one of the key reasons why taking massive action toward a goal creates so much powerful momentum that even limiting thought processes can't stop you.

Breathwork and Physiology: In my experience the fastest way to gain control of my emotions has always been through my body. What I mean by this is that when chaotic things are going on around you it will always come back to the following steps:

1. Take a deep controlled breath. A good diaphragmatic breath is best. Inhaling and exhaling at a controlled pace.
2. Move your body into a posture of power and confidence.
3. Interject a thought of power, something as simple as, "I got this," or, "I always find a way," "be aggressive", "this is great – you were made for this!", or, "This is just here to teach me something. I always find the solution."
4. Start asking better questions to redirect your entire frame of thinking to serve you better.

- What is good about this?
- What insight have I not seen...yet?
- Who has already solved this? Done this? If they can do it, so can I!

Taking control of your breathing and body movement sends the signal to your body's fight-or-flight system that it can stand down. Reminding yourself, "I'm good and I can handle whatever is going on," puts you back in the driver's seat.

Advanced Stuff: Have you ever heard the term, "be the Observer"?

I usually hear it in reference to meditation practices, but it can be a powerful filter too. Essentially it means having the flexibility of mind that you can see yourself from a third-party perspective *and* from your own first-person perspective at the same time. It's a great tool for getting out of your own head.

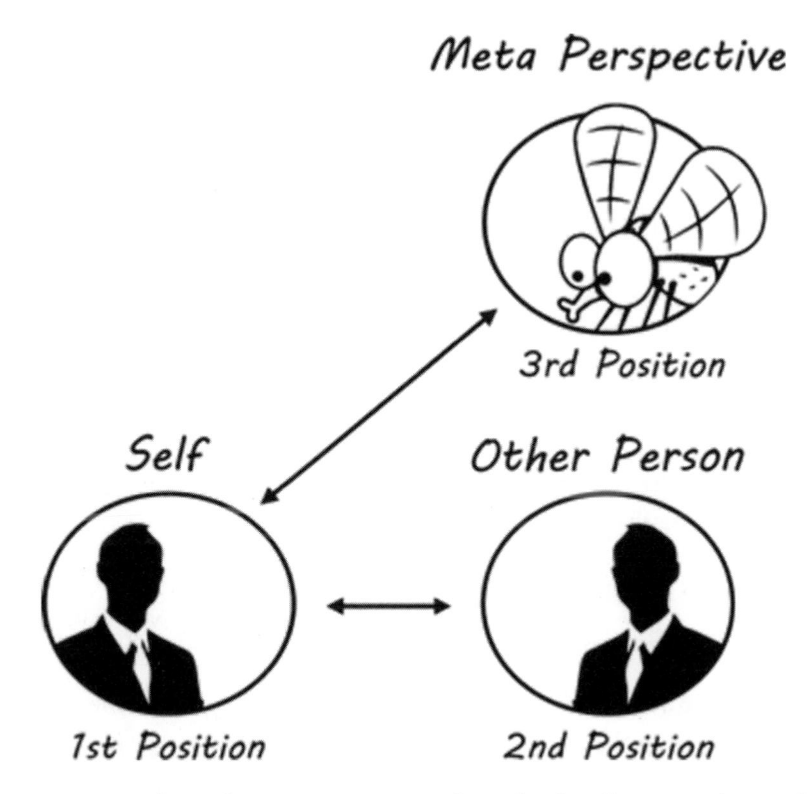

For example, right now you are reading this book. As you're reading these words you are probably looking at the page through your own eyes. You are "Associated" and immersed in the present moment.

Now, imagine you were looking at yourself reading the book. You would then be looking at yourself from a third-party perspective, and you would be removed from the act of reading. We call this being "Disassociated." Some call this a "meta-perspective."

Disassociation is a great tool for getting yourself out of a debilitating emotional state—something that would DEFINITELY be slowing down the momentum of your directional pull—because it allows you to step back from a high-stress situation or make a big decision from a non-emotional perspective.

One pattern I notice that debilitates people's ability to "think" clearly, quickly, and perform at a high level is that they "hang on" to past negative interactions too much. Or if they screwed something up, they don't "let it go" and put it behind them.

This is where Disassociation can be REALLY handy.

Let's take an example of something someone said to you that is bothering you when you think about it.

Step 1: Think of a time someone did or said something that still bothers you when you bring it up.

Step 2: Notice: are you associated (looking through your own eyes)? Or disassociated (watching yourself)?

My guess is that if it's bothering you, you are associated.

Step 3: Pop yourself out of the memory and shrink it down in size.

Once you've shrunk it down, keep yourself staying out of the memory and ask: has your feeling changed or did it completely go away?

Step 4: Here are a couple other fun things you can do with memories or people that have irritated you in the past:

- Shrink the person down in your mind to the size of a mouse.
- As they say their words, turn their voice into a Mickey Mouse tonality.
- Take an imaginary eraser, and erase their mouth. So, if they are trying to be mean, their words don't come out. (This is in your mind!)
- Take the memory, turn it into a coin, and watch it fly off into the sun.
- If the memory tries to come back, have it hit a trampoline and go back to the sun where it gets dissolved.

Step 5: If the person in the memory is from an influential person in your life and you'd like to have a good, long-lasting, useful memory, then do this:

5A: Ask yourself, what resources would that person need to have in order to make a good positive comment, suggestion to me?

I've found that most people are doing the best they can with the resources they had at the moment. If something went screwy, it wasn't because of you. It was them and their lack of ability in handling a situation.

If they had better capabilities, they would have behaved differently. Does that make sense? Most people who project out power, authority, and do it in a hurtful way are lacking many resources whether they know it or not.

Resources like confidence, patience, understanding, kindness, creativity, or a longer perspective to name a few. Think about what the person in the memory could have used.

5B: Then, from a Disassociated view, go 15 minutes (or even a full day) before the event ever happened and give the person all the resources they would have needed in this or any other situations in order to have behaved differently.

5C: Now, with these resources available to them, notice how differently they acted, spoke, and behaved moving forward.

5D: Re-run the memory with all these resources in place for everyone involved and notice how differently the experience is.

What's awesome about this simple process is you can apply it to unlimited amounts of areas in your life where you or others could have used more resources in order to behave differently.

6: Take The New Experience and Project It Forward!

Now, notice how the rest of your interactions with that person in the past re-evaluate themselves. They might change, you may get more awareness, and your power can come back. And as you look out into the future, with these new resources, notice what else is possible.

So where else can you apply this?

The possibilities are endless!!!

Up until now, you most likely have been approaching problems or opportunities with your current worldview. This is based on your identity, your values, and your belief systems of what's possible or not possible, your emotional states and experiences—all of which, as we just saw, you are capable of reshaping and redefining. You have the ability to bend your filters and, in doing so, bending your reality.

The next step is to experience your reality from new "perceptions" (we've already started this with our discussion of associated/disassociated views) and from different timelines (past, present, future). This is a huge key to Time Collapsing.

In a moment, we are going to walk through a couple exercises so that you can process this, but first let me talk about our perception of time and how you can use it to support you by removing negative trauma from your past and installing future goals and visions into your future.

BIG IDEA #2: Understand Your Relationship to Time

How do you organize time?

I don't mean how you schedule your day or how many weeks you are from taking a vacation. I'm talking about how you hold time in relation to where you're standing at any given moment.

Think about it this way: Point to your future. (Yes, take your hand and point to it.)

Are you pointing straight ahead of you? To your right? Above your head? Now point to your past. Are you pointing at your feet? Behind you? Where is your present? Point to it.

The directions you've chosen are not good or bad (though, as we're about to see, they do have meaning). What's amazing is that you had an answer to begin with! **The reason you had an answer to my questions is that we unconsciously organize our time awareness in space around us.**

Now, I want to go over a few more distinctions to lay some groundwork.

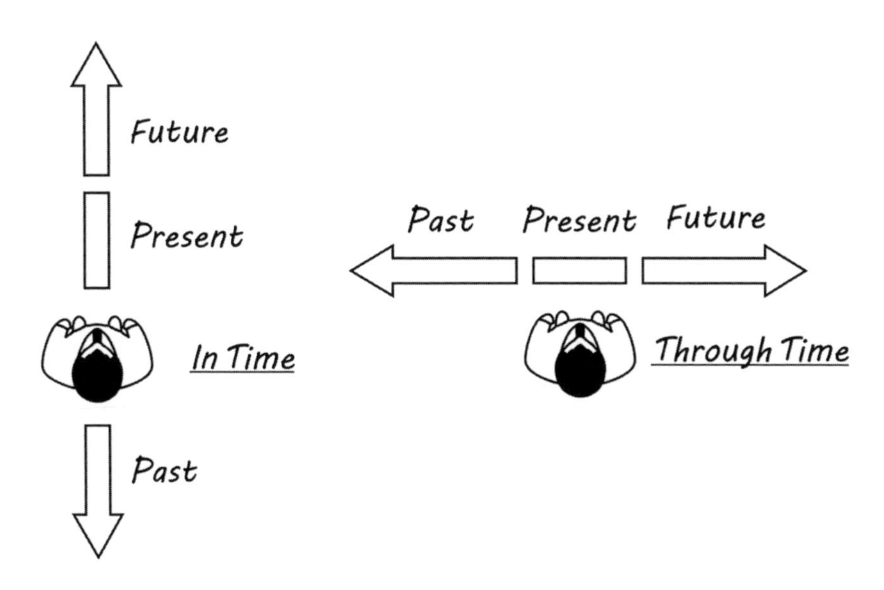

If you pictured your timeline running through you—meaning you pointed to your future straight ahead, and your past straight behind—you experience the present moment as if you are in it.

We call that being "In Time."

If you pictured your timeline running left to right out in front of you, you experience the present moment as if it is outside of you. That is what we call "Through Time."

People who are "In Time" tend to share certain characteristics:

- They lose track of time because they are so immersed in what they are doing.
- They often run late or get behind schedule.
- They are very connected to their emotional states and can be impacted by them.

People who are "Through Time" tend to have these characteristics:

- They can be very well organized.
- They have a good sense of their progress.
- They can pull things together without emotion.

The reason I share these characteristics is so that you understand how your personal sense of time works. Understanding how you live in time allows you to organize it according to your needs.

Yes, time itself is flexible! Your job is to find out how to utilize it more effectively and put time to work for you!

Here's an example of how to use these tools to solve problems differently. Think of a problem you are currently looking to solve. As an example, let's say you need to overcome a hurdle that is preventing you from taking your idea to the market. Or your next career decision.

Since we are talking about Time Collapsing, let's pick something that, if solved, will have a tremendous effect on speeding up where you want to go by 2-10X.

Maybe you have a lot of opportunities coming at you and you are deciding where to focus, but not "clear" on where you would like to go.

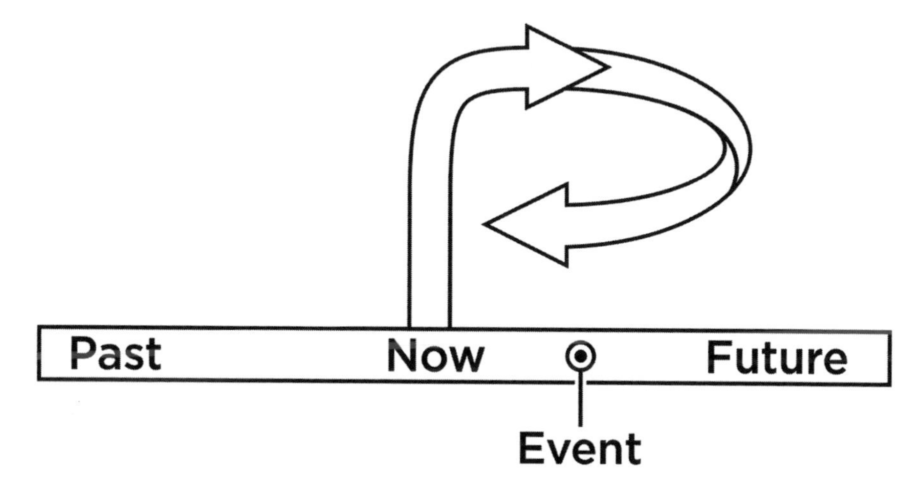

First, determine the problem. Right now, What is the problem?

What is *not* the problem?

How do you see the problem in your mind?

Picture your problem, and answer these questions. Keep it simple!

- Is your picture on a big screen, or a small one?
- Are you associated to it (meaning you are looking through your own eyes), or are you disassociated (are you seeing yourself in the image/movie)?
- Is it 2D, like a photo, or a 3D projection?
- Is it like looking at a movie, or like a still image?
- Is it in color, or is it in black and white?
- What feelings are you experiencing?

Now try taking the exact opposite perspective.

- If you pictured a big screen, make it smaller. If it was on a small screen, then make it bigger.
- If you viewed the problem from your first-person associated perspective, pop out of the picture and become disassociated.
- Did you picture a still image? Turn it into a movie. Or turn your movie into a still image.
- Black and White? Make it color. Turn color into black and white
- What happens if you turn it upside down?
- Put it behind you and look back at it, as if it is in your past. How does that look?

By doing these "silly" exercises, you are simply creating flexibility and opening up your filters to SEE more.

If you float out past the problem being 100% solved and look back at your journey, what do you now notice had to have happened in order for everything to come together?

IDENTITY How do you now see yourself in relationship to the old problem and newfound solutions?

BELIEFS. What is it that you would have to believe in order for this to have been solved and to now be your biggest asset and opportunity?

Notice how differently you feel with everything already being handled perfectly.

Key point: Do you notice that we flew out in the future, PAST the problem. This mentally and emotionally releases you at a conscious and unconscious level to have access to information and awareness that being "stuck" in the present moment won't allow you.

People "hold" all their limitations and perceptions about their limitations about the past, present and future...in the present moment. In order to free up your mind, you need to build this flexibility of the mind.

Now, it's time to lay some of the tracks from this new perspective.

Stay out in the future beyond the problem already being solved. Put your focus on what allowed you to accomplish your goal much faster than you ever thought. Ask yourself the following:

- Who is there?
- What key lessons did you learn?
- How did you execute?
- What were the key benchmarks in time that you notice?
- Is this what you truly want? Now that you have seen what the accomplishment of the goal looks like, are there any adjustments to the goal that you need to make?
- What are your loved ones? How are they responding to you? How much time are you spending with them? Is there anything you want to change?

Take 5-10 minutes to write these key awarenesses out. Get as specific as you can.

If you find that you can see what the future solution looks like, but the "How to's..." are still a little fuzzy, don't sweat it. ***You've opened up the doorway of possibility so your unconscious mind can start working on this. You have set your brain free to see your problem as something solvable!*** Wow!

BIG IDEA #3: Make a New Decision About Your Past To Accelerate Your Future

People tend to make long term pervasive decisions about themselves, about their capability, what is possible, and beliefs about what they've got going in their lives (business, relationships, sports, marriage, parenting, finances, career, etc.) because of an event in their past.

In a moment, I'm going to ask you to identify a limiting judgment or belief you have of yourself that stems from a decision you have consciously or unconsciously made about yourself. Most of these were handed to you by others or conclusions you have come to because of an experience or two.

KEEP THIS LIGHT! Stay disassociated as well. This exercise is not intended to used to "feel" bad, instead to create awareness to then have a breakthrough. So, pick an area you'd like to experience more options, desire to feel better, or have a breakthrough.

So what do you tell yourself?

Here are some self-limiting beliefs I've felt in my own life:

"I gain weight as I age." I remember someone close to me tell me at the end of high school that I'd start gaining weight. Well, I played volleyball for four years in college, trained hard, and stayed pretty lean.

After college, I wasn't perfect, but I ate somewhat healthy, worked out and kept the weight off. As I got older, became a parent, and I remember it was around age 32 that I was putting a little weight on. But it was "okay" and normal, because "people gain weight as they age." Right?

Wrong! I was experiencing tons of chronic fatigue. I decided to have my blood work, saliva, and urine analyzed by an integrative medicine doctor. He told me I had Adrenal Fatigue. I was hypersensitive to dairy and wheat, along with and a few other foods.

So, I cut those two out considerably. Stopped drinking beer and switched to wine. I lost 13 pounds pretty quickly, and I was lean once again.

Today, we eat mostly gluten-free. I still enjoy pizza and some "bad food" when I want, but 90% of the time I stick to eating healthy. And I still train five days a week.

What's my point? If you eat stuff that makes you fat, you'll get fat. If you don't move your body and train it, it will become a by-product of what you put in it and what you do with it. Age does not override those factors.

My belief was false.

"I'm a poor leader as a CEO." I like to create. I like creating marketing, writing books, and building out strategy. If I take on activities and roles inside my company that someone else would be better suited to do just because I'm "CEO," then I will feel like a failure. On the other hand, if other people organize the schedule of meetings and help set the agenda, I'm very good at sharing vision, giving the strategy, and working with team members.

So, I adjusted my belief: I am not a poor leader, but I wasn't creating the environment, vision, team members, and right alignment with my team. Once that is in place, I'm actually a great leader.

"I don't know how to make money." In my 20's. I was so focused on being "great" as a speaker and NLP practitioner/transformation coach that I was stumbling as an entrepreneur. I formed the belief that it was me personally that didn't know how to make money.

This was silly. Once I learned marketing, copywriting, and target marketing, I started the process of "making money". It became a simple Cause and effect relationship. If do "X" well, then "Y" shows up.

The belief (or beliefs) you've written down is going to be the focus of this section. We will work on creating a new and empowering decision that will OPEN UP YOUR FUTURE TO NEW POSSIBILITIES. Let's go!

Here's how we tackle your limiting beliefs.

Identify a limiting pattern that keeps showing up in your life. This is what you just did by listing out your limiting belief above.

Next, **verbalize or write out what you think the limiting decision was that you made to solidify this pattern.** What I mean by this is there came a point in your life when, after the event occurred, you decided that it meant something about you. For example, you may have launched an unsuccessful marketing campaign—that's the event—but at what point did you determine that it meant that marketing isn't your strong suit?

Now, **think back to when you have made your best decisions.** Set Step 2 aside for a second. Before we can go and make a new decision, one thing you need to "get" at a core level is that you already know how to make great decisions. Sometimes it's just a matter of taking that strategy, feeling, and thinking and placing it in the other context.

- What are the best decisions you've made in your life?
- How have they positively impacted you?
- Who helped you make those decisions?
- What have you learned since making them?

Okay, let's go back to your limiting beliefs. **We're now going to break free from time again**—just like we did in the last exercise. Float back to your decision point, the first time that you internalized the "meaning" of the event as signifying something limiting or negative about you.

Now, move into a third-party "Observer" position and look at that event and that decision with your new thinking—knowing what you know now, what lessons are there that you can see, hear, and feel? ***Knowing what you know now, how would you decide differently?*** Then, notice how all your judgements, decisions, and beliefs change from that point moving forward.

As you move forward, coming all the way back to the present moment, notice how many choices, events, and decisions have re-evaluated themselves ... and how many more options you are now that you are free of with these new points of view.

Finally, **look toward your future!** Take these new learnings and fly out to one month from now, three months from now, and six months and beyond noticing how differently your future is with this new empowering pattern and strategy, and system.

THE BEST WAY TO INCREASE YOUR ENERGY AND HAPPINESS INSTANTLY!

Now the next thing to try out is this:

From this high perspective, go to the part of your heart that holds the most gratitude and thankfulness for your life.

This might be your health, your family... ANYTHING.

I immediately thought of our baby twins and our 3.5 year old daughter, because their smiles and laughter bring joy wherever we go.

It might be something totally different for you.

Once you find that place, move into it. You may want to actually stand up and move around, to open up your body so you can actually feel this, because we need the feeling in your body before we move on. Maybe write down the 3-5 things you are most thankful for right now.

Once you are ready, from your heart send the grateful, thankful and joyous energy around the globe allowing it to light up everything it touches. And then envision that energy flowing back to you safely with great abundance...then touch down to where you live in this world.

There are no limits from this space. There is enough time. There is more than enough money. There are more than enough people. Everything is possible.

Ask yourself: In this space...is there anything here that you can't have or don't have? If you can think of something, simply add it.

Then, ask yourself this question: If I knew with 100% certainty that I had all of this and more as I went out in the world to pursue my passion, what would that feel like?

Take a minute to really infuse those feelings into every cell of your body, and then send that accumulated feeling around the world like you did in the initial gratitude exercise.

Doing this exercise and seeing yourself and the world through a different view is just one way to realize that you are connected to all the resources you desire. Nothing is beyond your reach. Everything you need is already here waiting for you to tap into them. What else might be possible?

Why These Tools Work

The goal of laying out the tools in this chapter was to show you how powerful your brain actually is and how FLEXIBLE reality can be once you know how to master your filters.

By looking at things from different points of view, with different perspectives, and putting old unresourceful decisions behind you while pulling new powerful decisions, beliefs, and strategies forward, you are creating an INCREDIBLY POWERFUL force in your service. You are on your way to being a Time Collapser!

Filters are so essential to this process for a number of reasons:

- In order to collapse time, you NEED to take control of what you want to see, want to believe, want to learn, and determine what means the most to you in your life.
- You MUST tell your brain exactly what you want it to seek out and create for you...and allow it to filter to you that information that will support you.
- CHOOSE the filters that will allow you to burst through the beliefs and traps that are holding you back.

Most motivational speakers talk about positive self-talk and visualization—that's all good, but it's too tactical. Core change that lasts forever and has dramatic impact should happen at the worldview/identity level.

Everything flows from that, so once that identity naturally shifts it all becomes easy. Best of all, there's no going back. After you've done this, your brain can't go back. It's like blowing up a balloon—it can never return to the size it was before.

The shortcut? Intentionally make an identity shift early and allow everything else to flow from there.

But Time Collapsing is not ***just*** about changing your perception; it is about actually achieving the things you want EXPONENTIALLY FASTER than most would believe possible. When you perform the exercises we discussed earlier—particularly the Gratitude Exercise—you will likely notice that you come out of it feeling physically better, lighter and more energized. That's no accident!

Higher energy levels are what make Time Collapsing possible!

Now, I'm not a quantum physicist. So if you are, please forgive this highly simplified explanation.

When we talk about raising energy levels, what we're actually talking about is speeding energy up. ***You see, you are a living, breathing energy magnet.*** One of the core principles of quantum physics is the idea that time is broken when energy accelerates; this happens because energy is atoms moving at an accelerated SPEED. When this occurs, the natural laws that we are traditionally accustomed to no longer exist.

We speed up our energy through high quality thought, emotion, and intention. Those are the keys to breaking the bonds of time!

Another way of looking at this is:

Imagine that the energy you are putting out in the world—the frequency at which your body, brain, everything are set—is on a scale of 0-100.

0 is the lowest of energy you can have, and 100 is the highest. And, for illustrative purposes, let's say 100 is divine/unconditional love for everything... and 0 is death. In between those two points, we have a whole spectrum of emotions that correspond to different energy levels.

Partial Map of the Scale of Consciousness

Self-View	Level	Log	Emotion	Process
Is	Enlightenment	700 - 1,000	Ineffable	Pure Consciousness
Perfect	Peace	600	Bliss	Illumination
Complete	Joy	540	Serenity	Transfiguration
Harmonious	Acceptance	350	Forgiveness	Transcendence
Feasible	Courage	200	Affirmation	Empowerment
Frightening	Fear	100	Anxiety	Withdrawal
Hopeless	Apathy, Hatred	50	Despair	Abdication
	Death	0		

On the lower end, we've got some of the nastier feelings: guilt, anger, helplessness, bitterness, clutter, chaos, frustration, guilt, approval seeking, shame and blame. On the high end, we've got the good stuff: enlightenment, joy, serenity, forgiveness, affirmation, acceptance and courage. Which end do you think will best serve your endeavors and overall quality of life? (Obvious question, I know...)

Imagine that there is a direct relationship with the energy level at which you're vibrating and the level of abundance you can experience. On which end of the energy spectrum would you want to set your thoughts, beliefs, emotional and physical states? (Yep, it's another obvious question...)

LISTEN CLOSELY: YOU CAN'T SUSTAIN LONG TERM ABUNDANCE IF YOUR ENERGY PATTERNS ARE CONSISTENTLY LOW.

With "broke" thoughts, come low energy action and intention... and the world boomerangs those thoughts, actions, and energy!

I see this very prevalently in the business and sports community. People work their butts off and raise their energy in an effort to make their first buck; then they finally pop some cash by learning a "trick" or system. They make a lot of money... and instantly lower their energy because they can "relax" now.

Imagine a person in the lower left hand of a page is giving off low energy and is surrounded by clutter. His low energy has pulled the clutter into his environment because they're operation at the same low level! The lower you go down that 0 to 100 scale, the slower you vibrate...and that means the things that you are pulling into your life will be sitting on a similarly low end of the scale.

Given what our little illustrated friend is pulling into his life, how could anything great ever happen?

You already know the answer to this, right? It can't. It won't. At least not while his energy is low.

Which brings us to...

Advanced Reality Bending!

Given everything that we've discussed in this chapter so far—filters of greatness, changing your perception, looking at your problems as though they're already solved—can you see how changing your filters and your emotional state into something very positive and exciting is the first step to actually *changing* your reality? I bet you can.

It's because by doing all those things, you are RAISING YOUR ENERGY LEVELS. As you consistently put these filters into practice, you won't have to think about them anymore because you will already be operating at a higher level. By continuing to put your consciousness on them, you can take yourself even higher, pulling in more and more positive or helpful "coincidences" that contribute to your growing Tsunami of Success!

There's another thing that happens too.

As you move up the energy ladder... the crowd thins out. It become easier the "breathe." And to gain more ***distinction.*** (And what is it that Time Collapsers are seeking?...)

Since you are a living and breathing magnet, and what you put out into the world comes back to you, your message, your signal is now able to be picked up by all the other people and resources that are resonating at that level.

- Customers who want to buy from you...
- Employees who want to work for you...
- A life partner who has all the qualities you are seeking...

- The resources you need...
- Mentors...
- Models...
- Ideas...

Is it this easy? Well, in many ways "YES"... and it might be even easier than I'm explaining.

Later in this book, I'll show you how to take your ability to bend reality and add actual strategies to leverage your new creative powers.

Chapter 7:

Find Your Superpower

Oh man, I could talk about superpowers all day. This part of the "process" never ends!

Dan Sullivan, from the Strategic Coach, said: "If you spend a lifetime working on your greatest weaknesses...you'll have a lot of better weaknesses." And I'll tell you, from personal experience, that is the TRUTH.

When I was 25 years old, I remember showing up at a meeting with my to-do list. 90% of the stuff on my to-do list had nothing to do with growing my business, making money, or achieving my goals. It was filled with things I didn't like doing, but "had" to do. For me that meant (as you know from the last chapter) any kind of logistical or organizational tasks.

One of my first mentors, Randy Davis, was the first person who told me that it's not only "okay," but that it's *vital* that YOU ONLY DO what ONLY YOU CAN DO!

What you are great at!

What you love doing!

This saying gave me permission to stop working on the things I suck at, to focus on identifying where my genius lies, and then work on expanding that area. If you concentrate on identifying your best strengths, the ones you enjoy using, and exercise those muscles… ***you can become one of the best in the world at that thing***.

The first step is identifying what Dan Sullivan defines as your "Unique Ability" in his Strategic Coach program:

"First, it is a superior ability that other people notice and value; second, we love doing it and want to do it as much as possible; third, it is energizing both for us and others around us; and, fourth, we keep getting better, never running out of possibilities for further improvement."

How can you recognize whether you are using your unique ability?

- It raises your energy.
- Time flies by when you do it.
- It seems to come to you natural and easy.
- If you never had to worry about money again, you'd probably do this thing.
- If you had to pay to do this all day, you would.
- If we asked the five people who know you best to describe what you are great at doing, what would they say?

My belief is that the best way to identify and cultivate your superpower is threefold: Life experience, tests, and trial and error.

Another way to figure out what your superpower might be is to do the following simple exercise. Start by drawing four squares on a piece of paper, and label them with the following:

LOVE, LIKE, DISLIKE, HATE. Then take stock of the activities you spend most of your time doing, and add them into the box they fit into best.

Once you place your activities in each box, you'll see a quick snapshot of your life.

When it comes to the things you "hate" doing, I predict you are also not "great" at them. They take you a long time to complete, and someone else could do it better than you.

"Like" and "Dislike" can be rather similar; the line between them can definitely blur. Sometimes you like things for a few years, then over time those activities drop into the "Dislike" category.

This happens a LOT after you've mastered something. When this happens, it's time to get someone else to do it.

I *LOVE* learning and acquiring new skill-sets. I *love* to identify the structure of how something works, and *like* figuring out something at least once.

But after I've seen it, felt it, and internalized it... I can move on.

Personally, my joy comes from the process of acquiring the skill. Not the ongoing process.

The idea behind this exercise is that it shows you how to dedicate your time and energy. You should spend most of your time on activities that ONLY fall in the LOVE and LIKE boxes.

Your goal should be to build a team or outsource ALL of the activities in your Dislike and Hate boxes, while eventually moving even the "Like" activities off your plate when you can. Here is why: the thing that you may dislike or hate will easily fall into the category of "Love" for someone else.

Another way to identify your unique abilities is to write out your Top 10 favorite things to do and things you love.

List Your 10 Favorite Things To Do!

The idea is this: this isn't just some run of the mill list of things you like. I want you to write this list out so honestly that if you didn't put your name on that piece of paper... and someone showed the list of activites it to your closest friends, they'd instantly know it was you.

Here's mine:

Ed's Love To Do List:

1. Creating in the form of writing or speaking on stage to an audience.
2. Coaching and teaching the game of volleyball.
3. Spending time with my wife and kids, Cuddling with my baby twins.
4. Daily Crossfit workouts or long Sealfit type workouts.
5. Brainstorming ideas of what is possible for my business or my clients businesses.
6. Having great conversation with people who inspire me (recording, creating, or listening to podcasts).
7. Watching Game of Thrones, Walking Dead, or some military or spy movie.
8. Reading.
9. Enjoying my coffee in the morning and a nice glass of wine on the weekends.
10. Watching my kids play sports.

List the Top People You Admire

Next, make a list of 3-5 people you admire, those whom you'd wish to model some of their behavior, outcomes, and results after.

What superpower do those people have that allows them to create such amazing results?

Do you feel a strong alignment to that superpower or something similar?

The purpose here is to simply have another way of piercing into what is your superpower. Write down your answers!

List What You'd Do With Unlimited Money, Time, and Resources

Assuming you had zero restrictions on your money, resources, or time, write down one thing you've always loved doing; something that you would do everyday if you could.

Big tip: if you can design your life as though you have no restrictions and build a cash cow that supports it, then you've already **created freedom** that even the wealthy never experience. Because YOU made it a key piece DURING your journey...so that when you hit your "walk away point" not much will change, because you're already living life exactly how you'd want to live it.

Align What You Love With Your Financial Freedom Vehicle

Once you've laid all these things out, it's just a matter of identifying who already has done something similar to it and follow the rest of the tools inside this book.

This potentially is the biggest misconception in our society!

The idea that you can live life on your own terms starting right now here regardless of your financial situation in create precisely what it is you want to do utilizing the thing that you're amazing at doing.

The more well-known people who in my perception are doing this are: Oprah Winfrey, JK Rowling, Stephen King, James Patterson, Adele, John Mackey (CEO of Whole Foods), Howard Shultz (CEO of Starbucks) , Elon Musk (Tesla), and many others.

This book is written around the idea that if you're ready to do something awesome, this is the time. The barrier to entry has never been lower. This includes cultivating your superpower.

Your current world is built in such a way to keep you as you are. Decide instead that you desire to live a life where your SUPERPOWER shines through and is developed. In the next section, we're going to take what we've learned so far and use it rocketship you ahead!

PART II:

The Time Collapsing Process

Attend Time Collapsing Mega-Conference LIVE!
"Real World, Multi-Million Dollar to Billion Dollar Entrepreneurs Share Their No-Holds Barred Approach For Hyper-Growth, Leaping To The Top, And Time Collapsing!"

Each year, we assemble an elite group of high performing entrepreneurs to share their "Time Collapsing" secrets for rapid success. You will learn advanced strategies that can only be taught by those who have been, in-the-trenches.

Whether you are starting, in a growth phase, or hitting a ceiling and looking for the slight edge, there will be something for you!

www.TimeCollapsingMegaconference.com

Time Collapsing Academy & Mastermind!
Get Personally Trained By Ed O'Keefe & An Elite Cadre of World Class Entrepreneurs!

You can get access to the highest level of real-world marketing, advertising, traffic, and sales processes with Time Collapsing Academy. An elite training program for entrepreneurs who are looking for rapid growth, more FREE Time, and truly wealthy life.

Time Collapsing Academy is the by-product of over 17 years of entrepreneurship experience, modeling best practices, and discovering the best way to accelerate all types of business models!

Find out what level of training is best suited for you at:

www.TimeCollapsingAcademy.com

Subscribe and Listen To Ed O'Keefe Show Podcast on Itunes!

Ed interview experts like: Jesse Itzler, Author of Living With A Seal! Jeff Usner: 50,000 Leads A Day Who Builds Houses and Schools For Orphans. Lewis Howes- Author of School of Greatness! Roland Frasier- Behind the Scenes Of Triple Digit Growth 3 Years In A Row! Com Mirza- Hear How Com sold his company for just under $500,000,000 after almost losing everything.

Plus, you can listen and watch Ed's Solo-Episodes Called The Time Collapsing Files!!!

www.EdOKeefeshow.com

Chapter 8:

LEAPFROG THEORY

The Leapfrog's Theory of Success is one of the fundamental, core success mindset shifts proposed in this book. It is what Time Collapsers use in order to say "goodbye" to the time limits imposed on us by society.

In Robert Ringer's book, *Winning Through Intimidation, the Leap Frog Theory States:*

No one has an obligation — moral, legal, or otherwise — to "work his way up through the ranks." Every human being possesses an inalienable right to make a unilateral decision to redirect his career and begin operating on a higher level at any time that he, and he alone, believes he is ready.

This realization was so impactful for me! It showed me that I didn't need to slowly work my way up the ladder, following in the footsteps of my mentors until "my turn" finally came. **Some people use the term "standing on the shoulders of giants."**

I like to use the term **"taking the elevator while everyone else takes the stairs."**

Conceptually, this is the core mindset shift: ***I do not need the approval of all these other people, the certifications, the degrees, or Professor Jones to give me his blessing. I can create my own path—and leap ahead.*** I no longer need to take the steps (Photo A), but can simply think and operate from the top (Photo B).

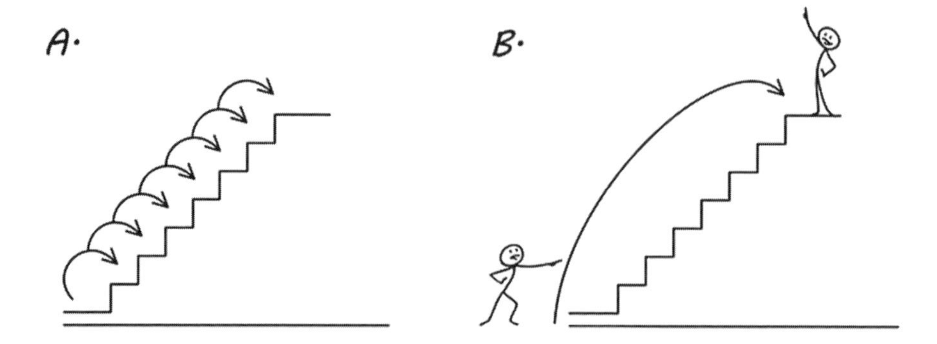

Imagine your life is on a whiteboard.

Wipe it clean and then write, draw, and create whatever you want and then go out and do it.

The other part of this formula as stated by Ringer is that if you're going to declare that you belong at the high tier you're choosing, then it's on you to make sure you're able to compete and deliver at that level. If you can't, you'll get knocked back down. I would suggest that you will probably get knocked down faster than you thought because of social media nowadays.

With that said, there are so many tools at your disposal to help keep you at high caliber. Every solution you need to provide a service, to fulfill something, and to support people is out there in the world. You can either hire it, barter for it, find it, or get it for free on YouTube or Google.

Let me give you some specific ways that I implemented Leapfrog Theory early in my career.

First, I started charging more. Let's say a company wants to hire you and you charge $125. What if you decided to charge $1,250? Instantly the perceived credibility is higher. Now let's do some basic math to see how this one move played out for me.

Before my price increase, let's say seven out of ten people were hiring me. I was extremely busy because I was offering cheap labor. But, despite my full calendar, I was on the treadmill and could barely pay my bills! Despite the fact that I was busting my ass, at the end of the day my total revenue generated was $875.

Once I raised my rate 10x, my workload went WAY down—one out of ten people were hiring me. This initially spooked me, but I soon realized the tremendous benefit of having so much time freed up. I could spend more time learning, identifying and connecting with mentors, and getting the right marketing to the right people.

By providing that one client with the good, quality service, I could now deliver more value and better service. It should come as no surprise that I was making more money taking on fewer clients with a higher rate.

It was the Leapfrog Theory at work!

Chapter 9:

Time Collapsing Money System

You can apply the Leapfrog Theory to every area of your life. In the coming chapters we're going to explore how you can implement it into the several key areas of Time Collapsing: **Money, Access, Authority, and Expertise**. Let's start with money.

We're kicking things off by putting you in the 1%.

According to the IRS, in 2014 it only took $159,619 to put you in the top 5% of income earners in the world. The top 1% was only $380,354.[4]

So, grab a pen and a piece of paper and write: "I happily earn $160,000 by providing awesome products or service **(insert your own thing here)** that transform people's lives worldwide."

Set your pen down and read it again. Use the same perspective-shifting techniques we learned earlier in this book to soak this sentence into your cells. Your brain starts to shift, doesn't it?

Now, pick your pen back up and add another zero, making the number $1,600,000.00. How does that feel? Notice how your brain shifts again.

[4] Source: Financial Samurai.com, Source/Daily Income

What feelings are showing up? What biases, beliefs, or thoughts are ringing between your ears? Are you feeling resistant to the idea that it's possible?

Thanks to the foundation we laid in the previous section, you now have tools to go back and change the beliefs that might be holding you back from thinking that the number on the page is attainable. **But there's another point to this exercise: testing out the limits of where your mind is currently willing to go, and finding out how far out you can get before your brain doesn't believe it's possible.**

So now that we've pushed your financial goals to their edge, let's revisit that original $160,000. What would it look like if we bumped it by just 30%? $208,000. How does that feel?

This simple exercise works very well. And it's the first step toward achieving the seven-figure number that feels like a reach right now.

A "structural tension" occurs when you state a goal or claim to something that has yet to happen. Don't see it as a roadblock, or as your brain slamming the brakes! Just because you're feeling that tension, doesn't mean that the achievement isn't possible. In fact, you can put it to good use as a catalyst of creativity. Use it to lift up your energy to that it contributes to the momentum of you directional pull!

Okay, now let's go back to that original $160,000 to look at how we can make it achievable.

For example, there are 12 months, 52 weeks, 365 days, and approximately 2080 work hours on average per person in a year—so let's just do the basic math.

	Income:	**Monthly** (12)	**Weekly** (52)	**Daily** (365)	**Hourly** (2080)
Top 3%	$160,000	$13,333	$3,077	$438	$76
Top 1%	$381,000	$31,750	$7,326	$732	$183

When looking at these numbers, you need to take into account a few assumptions:

1. These are **pre-tax numbers;** which means you're spending capability is NOT your income. You need to calculate taxes and fees to get your actual spending power.
2. **I used 365 days.** However, I NEVER plan on working that much and don't expect you to either. If you focus on dividing your income by "actual work days," then the average number is 261. This will increase your daily "target" by 28% per day.

With that in mind, the next step is to look at what Wealth Vehicle can get you there. Your wealth vehicle is "how you make money." This could be a job, a business, or an investment vehicle.

If you're building a business, you have one other decision point:

A. Am I growing this business in order to sell it and get one big payday?

or..

B. Am I growing this business to be a great cash cow, so I can build my wealth through my distributions being invested over a period of time?

For me personally, I'm assuming that these numbers will be hit through a business "system" I create that works <u>without my daily presence.</u> This is how I think about building and creating leverage. Then the cash flow off that will be invested and over time increase value. Other leverage points include:

- An author, speaker, or even actor may be looking at leverage through speaking, seminars, movies. These can be big pay days.

- Podcastors must focus on downloads and listenership. They can be leveraged through getting paid by sponsors, promoting other people's products as an affiliate, creating their own products, or as a tool to get equity in businesses in exchange for promotion.
- Content media platforms might focus on visitors, average pages viewed, and earnings per 1000 Visitors (ecpm) through advertising.
- A hybrid model where you get one or all of these things is becoming more and more prevalent now that content marketing, social media, virality, ecommerce, AND publishing (books or podcasts) can be something YOU can do without any permission from anyone.
- Then there is the Investor! A person who invests in assets, like a business, real estate, stock, or other opportunities may set the goal that paying $1 today, which then will increase in value over time while the asset does the "work."

In our society today, whether you know it or not, everyone is an entrepreneur when it comes to money. You just need to figure out where you fit in, how to create enormous value, do the math, and find your leverage.

Then you have to manage your TIME accordingly.

With your yearly earnings number in mind, break it down to an hourly rate. This is your TARGET to hit hourly when working on activities—and anything that doesn't directly contribute to hitting that target must go. For example, if you desire to make $100/hour or $1,000 an hour, you need to take EVERYTHING that earns less than that dollar amount and have someone else do it. No more cutting your own grass, shopping for food, gardening, or activities that don't support your target goal.

Of course, there are a few exceptions to this rule:

- You LOVE those activities so much they are part of your rejuvenating process. (If you're passionate about mowing your lawn, please don't let me stop you.)
- You are in building phase of something. You are building out a sales process, a marketing campaign, or doing research. Those activities may take TIME, whereby you are losing money every hour you spend on them, but you understand that these activities (when they come together) will provide exponential LEVERAGE.
- You are building the business to hit a certain SCALE that fires off highly leveraged cash flow and value once you hit it. The immediate work will have a perceived lack of "profit," however, it is HIGHLY valuable and should be treated as such.

Now, as we've learned in the previous chapters, doing the math is important but it isn't enough. You've got to set your brain—your filters, belief systems, and superpowers—to Time Collapsing mode.

TAKING YOUR LEAP FROG GOALS AND MAKING THEM REAL!

Step 1: State How Much You Desire To Make:

I am happily earning ____________________, by (*insert how you plan to create value*) by (*insert date*).

"I am enthusiastically earning $300,000 a year by buying family homes and renting them to great families in my neighborhood by December 31st (insert year)."

Step 2: Break it down: Take the figure you listed above, and start breaking it down into steps.

$1,000,000

You need 5,000 people to buy a $200 product
You need 2,000 people to buy a $500 product
You need 1,000 people to buy a $1,000 product
You need 500 people to buy a $2,000 product
You need 300 people to buy a $3,333 product

Get 5,000 people to pay $17 per month, for 12 months
Get 2,000 people to pay $42 per month, for 12 months
Get 1,000 people to pay $83 per month, for 12 months
Get 500 people to pay $167 per month, for 12 months
Get 300 people to pay $278 per month, for 12 months

$1,000,000 in profit would require $83,333 in profit per month.

You can use the example above, or use your own figure and wealth vehicle to answer the following questions:

- How many new customers and existing repurchasing customers would you need in your business?
- How many homes would you need to own and have rented?
- What is your target value per customer?
- The Number of leads to get a new customer? What is your conversion rate?
- How many speaking engagements? Webinars?

Step 3: Break this down into Profit Centers, Revenue Targets and Customers By Source!

You can now break it down into profit centers or product lines. If you are just starting or want to keep it simple, then just pick one profit center, revenue source, product line, or line of work.

Don't stress this out. Have fun with it!

Also, one more point: as you are starting out, you can do some basic conservative estimates. When we buy any kind of advertising or spend money on marketing, we will do a ton of research to find out industry norms or competitor averages. Then compare our first campaign against this.

The goal is to determine a baseline so you know where to improve!

If you already have data, it doesn't need to be perfect. **Just get a baseline.**

Step 4: Break it down even more:

Revenue Source and Revenue Goal: $____________

Product Price (Average) $___________

Target Revenue/ Product Price = # of Sales Needed

How many sales do you need? #___________

Conversion Rate? (# of Sales/# of Leads/Visitors) #___________

(Conversion rate is the percentage of people who buy divided by the number of leads or the number of visitors to your site. Downloads from your podcast. Book buyers...)

#of Sales Needed/Conversion Rate= # of Leads Needed.

# of Leads Needed: #____________

Cost Per Lead: #____________

Monthly Required Ad Spend to Hit Target: $__________

Then apply this math to each source of leads and customers to see where you can expand.

80/20 Your Most Profitable Sources, Customers, and Investment!

Let's talk about the "80/20 Rule." This rule, also known as the Pareto Principle, is the key to efficiently dedicating your time and energy to the things that are going to help you hit your target.

The Pareto Principle, sometimes referred to as the 80/20 Rule or the Rule of the Vital Few, states that 20 percent of your client/client base will be worth 80 percent of your profits—and 20 percent of your client base will be the cause of 80 percent of your headaches, but that's a different story for a different day.

The 20 percent worth 80 percent of your profits deserve far more time and attention (and financial investment) than the flagging 80 percent that only produce 20 percent.

But you can't focus on your best 20 percent if you don't know who they are. Who are your MVC's (Most Valuable Customers)??

In Time Collapsing, separating out what is NOT VITAL is sometimes more important than knowing every essential. This principle holds true for how you spend your time, the employees you hire, vendors, strategic relationships, customers, mentors, and so much more.

The ratio may vary, but there is ALWAYS a vital few that makes the majority of the difference.

This leads us to our next steps...

Step 5. Challenge Your Assumptions of Your Plan

Push yourself back out to the boundaries of your thinking with the following questions:

- What would need to happen to accomplish this goal in half the time (6 months)?
- What would need to happen to accomplish this goal in 90 Days?
- What would need to happen to accomplish this goal in 30 Days?

- What if we did 2X more than we expected? What would have to happen to make that achievable?
- What else is possible?
- Where else might my Time Collapsing System apply?

Step 6: Where is the Limiting GAP You Need to Fill to Make the Leap?

Now, you need to find the GAP between where you currently are and where you want to be with this plan.

This usually falls into the following areas:

I have the wrong wealth vehicle. Some of my biggest leaps have come when I've realized, "I'm in the wrong business," or, "This profession sucks." When I was running my first business selling mental toughness manuals and videos to athletes and coaches, I did this exact "math" exercise and realized I was selling to people who didn't have money in a limited marketplace. That was the key decision point to which eventually led me to going into the dental marketing business.

In hindsight, it was a no-brainer, but at the time it was extremely difficult mentally and emotionally. The faster you can fly through that friction, the better off you will be. Making a pivot in your plan is not the same as "giving up." Pivoting can be a mature approach to business. Relentlessly trying to pound a business past the goal line without a plan that has any mathematical hope is insanity.

You may be in the right business, BUT your realization might be....

- **"I'm running my business wrong!"** This could stem from a series of things: the market you're targeting, the product, your pricing, etc...but those are all strategy things. If you have the right strategy in place, you probably are either: **no longer using your superpower or doing "too much."**

- **"I'm lacking a key skill or specialized knowledge."** Since we live in such an evolving time where information is changing so rapidly, it is impossible to stay on top of what is exactly working for every media, process, and skillsets.

  My first breakthrough happened when I heard a speaker say: "Your income is directly correlated to your ability to write sales copy!" Well, I started practicing copywriting like my life depended on it. He was right, the better I was able to write sales copy the more money I made. But to this day, new problems arise and I have to learn new skillsets. **THIS *ongoing and never-ending* process of acquiring multiple specialized skillsets IS the secret to success in a business.**

  Simply by DOING these exercises, even if you don't see the path and plan, you force your mind to expand and start seeing resources, mentors, and pathways that weren't there before.

The Final Step: Now, you want to take this plan you have laid out and get someone who already has it figured out to give you some input. This is why the Time Collapsing Academy is so powerful!

I guarantee you that your plan, as daunting, exciting, or challenging as it may sound, seems easy to someone else. You want to get THAT person's feedback, perspective, and filters.

Which leads us nicely into the Time Collapsing Power Relationship System!

Chapter 10:

POWER RELATIONSHIPS!

Simon Black likes his privacy and absolutely hates talking about himself personally. Thus why he uses a pseudonym for his highly insightful and controversial newsletter sovereignman.com. Billionaires and multi-deca millionaires seek him out for advice as the "international man."

My favorite of all his reports was titled: "Network Infiltration! The Secrets To Becoming A Welcomed Member To The Most Exclusive Networks In The World."

This isn't typical "networking" that is used by most sales people and most business men and women. As he writes, networking is an evolutionary process where you expand your network, while network infiltration is a deliberate approach that gives you a quantum leap in the quality, value of relationships and all associated opportunities!

There's a massive difference between being *connected* and being *influential* with the right circles of influence, power, knowledge, and capability.

Black made this discovery almost by accident. After making some money with a great business and passive income he set out not in search of power, but in search of adventure. He found both. He describes it:

"I started in Panama...first meeting some successful young attorneys, real estate agents, and developers. They introduced me to their friends, their friends' friends, etc., and eventually I was having drinks with some of the wealthiest people in the country."

He realized that one of his best sources in getting connected and building an influential network came from identifying a well-connected attorney. In his own words, "a good attorney has a little black book that is more valuable than his entire practice. A great attorney doesn't need one."

When entering a new area or new country, his first step is to find a highly connected attorney. Black stays in the nicest hotel, a way of suggesting he has money. He explains to the receptionist that he is an international investor and interested in meeting with some of the partners about making investments in that country.

After a few filtering questions and criteria (which, if you're interested in learning, I highly recommend you read the full report), he will say: "Okay, lets meet at your office at 3:00 pm. Please send a car at 2:30 sharp." This is another posturing and pre-qualification strategy. If they don't have a car, it means they aren't as luxury as he thought, and he can cancel the meeting.

During the meeting, he will ask more questions to make sure he is dealing with the right people and that they are connected. Then he gives a very broad personal background that draws interest and differentiates himself from others. At the end of the meeting, he leaves a nominal offer to retain this group.

Paying to Play

What is key to understanding Black's system—and understanding the Time Collapsing Power Network vehicle—is that it might only cost $1,000 to $5,000, but you NOW have ACCESS. Understanding this component of getting access is key. To Time Collapse, you need to understand that paying to get access is much better than showing up with your hand out begging.

Under his system, Black will be invited as a guest to dinner within a few days where he will be introduced to other people of influence. People who have networks. In the report, he refers to these people as "nodes."

A node is an individual who can **open doors for you to a specific network**. The first step in getting "connected" would be to have a reason. Then to identify the network you would like to either influence or join. In each of these groups, you need to look for the person who opens the doorway. That person is...THE NODE.

The lawyer was the first node for Simon Black. The next might be someone who has a network of real estate sellers and gives him (and his inner circle) first right of refusal to certain deals.

Get access to a node and you get access to their network. It is a constantly evolving and never ending means of growth.

Why Everyone Needs A Power Network

You may be thinking, "But Ed, I'm not an international investor! This doesn't apply to me!"

Listen closely: You can be talented, attractive, successful, or whatever attribute you'd like to have, but I'm not sure if there is a more powerful attribute than to build relationships with people who can rocketship you to the next level.

Whether it's a mentor, someone who is world-class at what they do, a celebrity, potential business relationship, teacher, a company that might buy your business, or anyone else, **you need to have a strategy for relationship building.**

Nothing happens without relationships!

Nido qubein, a famous author, businessman, and president of High Point University since 2005, once said: "Access is Power," and, "Who you spend your time with is who you become!"

Harvey McCay, author of *Swim With The Sharks Without Getting Eaten Alive!* And *Dig Your Well Before You Are Thirsty!* states:

> "A network replaces the weakness of the individual with the strength of the group. The idea of the group is to benefit members who have the same race, religion, gender preferences, ethnic background, business, trade and professional interests, economic interests, or personal interests. They are the basic building blocks of any networking system."

Harvey was famous for creating best-selling books by simply keeping in touch with every friend and customer. When he launched a book, they would all buy it. *Dig Your Well Before You Are Thirsty!* walks sales reps and entrepreneurs through his process of cultivating and keeping loyal friends and customers.

With that in mind, let's dig into how we can use the Leapfrog Theory to gain access to individuals or groups by building your Power Network.

What Relationships Can Support You Best?

Step 1: Building Your Power Network With 2, 3, 5, 20, 100,1000

Let's start by taking a look at the kinds of people and relationships you want to build into your life. Here is a framework that I think about when looking at my power network:

2 Models: Since Time Collapsing requires the concept of modeling (a concept we will be discussing in depth later in this book), my belief is that you should have one or two, but no more than that. (Even three can get cluttered.)

3 consultants, mentors, or advisors: Just like a professional athlete will have coaches who specialize in different aspects of the sport, it's impossible to be an expert at all areas. Early on, you may start with one mentor, but your job is to surpass your mentors, not stay static. I like having multiple perspectives when making decisions. To me, three is perfect.

5 People You Can Be Naked In The Shower With!: I don't mean literally getting in the shower with these folks, but you need to have five people with whom you can be completely transparent, or "naked." These are the people you can call and tell them the most embarrassing, stupidest mistakes that you have made and they won't judge you. They accept you for your gifts, but more importantly can still accept you and support you even though you have faults.

20 Mastermind Partners: In his book, *Think and Grow Rich,* Napolean Hill has made the concept of the mastermind group, a small circle of people who support each other's plans and a must-have for all people who are looking to create big things in this world. Dr. Hill defines it as, "a mind that is developed through the harmonious cooperation of two or more people who ally themselves for the purpose of accomplishing any given task." I would also define it as the seed of your Power Network.

I created the Time Collapsing Academy and Mastermind to create a powerful network of people who are doing amazing things. The idea behind a mastermind is that 1 + 1 doesn't make 2; thanks to synergy, it makes 11. If you don't have a Mastermind group, visit Time Collapsing Academy and see if it's a fit for your goals.

100 Strategic Partners: if you have a good product or service, podcast, book, or media platform, then people should be raving about you and promoting you. Whether it's 10 or 100, or 1000, you must have a plan for getting people to promote you. Whether it's through word of mouth/goodwill, affiliate promotions, joint ventures, partnership, or licensing, this is a long term strategy that will build your wealth. Like all other things, you need to be able to create more value for them than you expect to receive.

1000 True Fans: No matter where you are in your entrepreneurial journey, you probably already have 1000 fans that are underappreciated right now. OR you are starting out and CAN hit 1000 fans through focus and value creation. Kevin Kelly states that the way to deal with "The Long Tail," the splintering of social media and the clutter and noise it creates, is to cultivate YOUR 1000 True fans.

As Kelly defines it: "A True Fan is defined as someone who will purchase anything and everything you produce. They will drive 200 miles to see you sing. They will buy the super deluxe re-issued hi-res box set of your stuff even though they have the low-res version. They have a Google Alert set for your name. They bookmark the eBay page where your out-of-print editions show up. They come to your openings. They have you sign their copies. They buy the t-shirt, and the mug, and the hat. They can't wait till you issue your next work. They are true fans."[5]

"But Ed," you might be thinking, "1,000 feels like a really small target." I hear you on that. Let me explain.

In *Zero To One,* billionaire and PayPal co-founder Peter Theil explained that PayPal focused on **a market as small as 20,000. They knew that if they could crack and dominate THAT group, they would be able to scale. But THAT group was the key focus!**

This is exactly what I'm suggesting you do. Too many people go broad too early and end up wasting time, resources, and potential relationships. Don't be one of them!

[5] "The Technium: 1,000 True Fans." The Technium: 1,000 True Fans. March 04, 2008. Accessed June 29, 2016. http://kk.org/thetechnium/1000-true-fans/.

Here is a short list of questions to get you "thinking" about who you might want to put on your list of people with whom you would like to build a relationship or gain access:

- What is the strategy? What are the skillsets that I must learn?
- What strategy am I not thinking of currently that would produce the same results?
- Who are the people who can help me with these questions?
- Who is already where I want to be?
- Who has tried what I want to do and failed? Or Quit? Or Pivoted out of it?
- Who are the happiest people I know of?
- Who are the wealthiest people I know of?
- Who seems to know how to win in anything they put their mind to?
- Who can help me promote my company?
- Who can I provide value to right now that is not already in my network?
- Who can give me qualified, honest, advice?
- Who can give me ridiculously genius level insight that can cut years off my learning curve?
- Which of my friends will help me toward my goal? Who will be honest with me and treat my goals with the same level of importance as I do?
- Who do I know has massive influence already, whose help would be equivalent to that of 1000 other people?

Step 2: Start With Yourself First!

There is nothing worse than to have an opportunity of a lifetime get introduced to you, but you failed to be prepared when it occurred. Don't let it happen to you!

Ask yourself: "What type of person must I be in order to attract these people into my life? What energetic pattern do I need to be living to naturally attract these people into my life?"

Listen closely: the world is smaller than it's ever been. You want your name, reputation, and overall character flowing out to all directions. Put some time and thought into answering these next two questions, as they will give you an assessment of where you currently are and help you define where you want to be:

- If your closest business and personal friends were to describe you in 20 seconds or less, what would they say about you?
- What would be your ideal introduction and description, that if told to everyone on your dream contact list would have them banging at your door to meet you? Do business with you? Support you 1000% unselfishly?

Step 3: Create a Boomerang Game Plan!

A core principle for everything Time Collapsers do is to *attract*! Never chase!

When most people are seeking access or a connection they are chasing, the interaction inevitably sounds like this: "Here's my card, let's get on call, grab coffee, try my service, hire me, do this..." Gag me.

Remember when you first met the super hot girl in high school. I do! I also remember running over to her every time I saw her. Trying to be nice. Trying to impress her. What do you think happened? She ended up dating the guy who completely ignored her.

It's a truth that took me way too long to discover that says ***the faster we chase something the faster it moves away from us***.

However, when we take the time to set up the circumstances to attract it, so much of it will fly towards you! This is true about relationships, customers, opportunities, and money as well.

By "attract," I'm not talking about law of attraction. I'm talking about getting the other side to move towards you. In my businesses, we use lead generation, direct response marketing, and Facebook video ads that enable us to get very targeted with who we want to watch our videos.

> TIP: the best ads don't look like "ads." They look like highly valuable content that helps people, and gets them moving to the next step because they WANT MORE!

We also take a lot of steps to build out our media platform via podcasts, blogs and, yes, books. Why should everyone who wants to have influence build a media platform, get on podcasts, and write a book? Our population equates that with influence, but also it allows people in networks that you want to connect with to FIND YOU! TALK ABOUT YOU! REACH OUT TO YOU!

Recently, my friend and world-class SEO and marketing expert was sharing his latest strategy that is skyrocketing conversion rates online: "The secret is that the person feels it was their idea to buy the product," that they weren't SOLD! The same is true with building your Power Network!

The typical way people approach others is with a harder, more direct approach:

- "I have this idea, project, or thing I'd like you to look at______!"
- "Can you give me your opinion?"
- "Can we get meetup for coffee, a beer, etc.?"

- "Can you introduce me to ______________________________?"
- They only contact an influencer when they want something

You may think that "being direct" is good, but to people who are successful, busy, and have limited time, it's a quick way to destroy any potential credibility that you might have. Instead of looking like a go-getter, you'll just look like you don't get it.

Step 3: Create Massive Value For Them.

Com Mirza is a an outstanding serial entrepreneur and investor who, on the brink of losing it all and being rejected by over 40 venture capitalists, finally hit a breakthrough before building that company and selling it for hundreds of millions of dollars.You can hear his full story in an interview I did with Com at www.EdOKeefeShow.com, but I wanted to highlight a story he shared about how he attracted his billionaire mentor. There are so many great lessons here:

> "I wanted to connect with a specific person a few years back, and **he didn't know who I was at all.** He had seen my face around at social and charitable gatherings but we had never connected other than the casual smile once in awhile.
>
> I wanted to reach out to him to connect to build a relationship and learn from him eventually. But I was actually afraid to reach out I actually felt fearful of him saying NO to my request. I've been told "No" almost all my life so I never let a no stop me. But with this guy I just couldn't even fathom a no. It would have crushed me a bit,because I was very passionate about him and it was like a business crush! I can't believe I'm sharing this! So instead of me potentially getting a no I said to myself, **"How can I get a yes!?"**
>
> Instead of befriending him I tried to befriend his friends. I made connections and relationships with people he hung around. I spent **<u>money and time</u>** and built up a ***good friendship with six of his friends.***

Slowly but surely they started to mention me at their own gatherings and this person would hear about me all the time.

He then came up to me at a charity event and he introduced himself while I was in a circle with some of his friends. I connected with him and inside I was thinking, "How do I get him away from this circle and talk to him?"

We broke the ice so I was anxious to build further. I wanted to scale this relationship and fast. But I couldn't find a way to do it. He was so busy and speaking with so many people I didn't think I would get proper time alone. So I kept my patience and played it cool.

I then ran into him a week later at another event, and we chatted briefly for five minutes. I wanted to invite him to dinner at my house in the Burj Khalifa but once again I was afraid of a NO from him. So bit my tongue and kept my patience again. I spent some money on charity stuff that day and further got his attention.

He ended up inviting me to a small gathering at his house and we finally connected. We chatted for 5 hours till 3:30 in the morning. We hit it off well and kept hanging around together in very small private settings. He ended up influencing my life in a great way as well as becoming one of my mentors in life. I paid a hell of alot for it in time and money (and am still paying for it) but he changed my life. Which I view as a priceless return on investment."

As Com came under the mentorship of his new billionaire friend, he began to notice a powerful change in himself. As he puts it, his mindset changed when in the company of his mentor, and that rippled out to cause his behaviors and actions to change as well.

"I became a machine of contribution, overly obsessing about it and also falling out from it due to frustration and burnout. He helped me come back to it more patient and understanding of how great a responsibility it is and only the chosen ones get to spread that message. But they are tested the most and that **they can't avoid their destiny and purpose.**"

Long story short, Com's billionaire mentor helped him make 9 figures in his business by unlocking his mindset and helping him realize his full potential and purpose!

So the lesson is ***don't be afraid to set your sights high. Don't be afraid to spend money and time to build that relationship, and don't be afraid of one way not working, try several ways and you will find the one that works.***

Step 3: Ask God to help you?

Whenever we lose things at my house, we say a prayer to St. Anthony. It works like magic.

Why wouldn't you ask your Angels, God, Spirit Guides, and the Universe to jump in and lend a hand? Say something as simple as:

"I know you know better than me who can help me attain this goal much faster than I can in order to provide exponentially more value to this world. Can you please have your Angels go out and talk to these people's angels and start the process of us connecting at light speeds?"

Have fun with this. Be open to the possibilities and doorways that are ready to open, but you MUST ask first.

Step 4: Cut the Fat, Chisel Your Armour:

Remember, iron sharpens iron. If you are preparing to meet super high-level black belts, but you are training once a week with white belts... well, you are kidding yourself. I wanted to interview Commander Mark Divine for my podcast and build that relationship, and that required me to literally cut the fat.

My strategy: go do his Kokoro Camp, the 50-hour Hell Week experience that is modeled on Navy Seal BUDS training—yeah, I was going to have to earn this connection with actual blood, sweat, and tears. After I did Mark's camp, it was easy to ask something small of him because I had just done what he trains men and women to do. It was the positioning I wanted.

When you look through your list, do an honest evaluation of yourself:

- If the people on your dream contact list showed up today, would you be ready to meet them, create value for them, and would they genuinely want to do business with you? Mentor you? Be a friend? Take your advice? Introduce you to their network?

If the answer is "no," then write down all the reasons you think they wouldn't.

Now ask yourself this: Can you change those things? Can you get rid of any relationships, limiting beliefs, businesses, or anything else that would free this blockage up? If it's a knowledge or skillset thing, don't sweat it, list out what you need to learn and get after it.

If the magic moment happens and you aren't fully prepared, don't sweat it. Just be yourself. **Always be yourself and always aim to provide value first**, even if you have a question or two.

For example, if you end up meeting them sooner than you'd like, let them know you have a goal of sharing something with them and would love their input when you are prepared. 95% of the time they are flattered and admire your excitement, honesty, and transparency.

Not everyone is going to be friendly, of course, but if you set the right intention and always take the frame as a Value Creator, things tend to work out. Now, if you add this Time Collapsing Power Network System on top of it...you are lights out ahead of everyone else!

If you don't click with one of your contacts, then that might be an indication of misalignment. Not everyone on your list will resonate with you, nor you with them. That's okay! Don't be attached to it. You are only creating your best "perception" as to who might be your magic list.

Life is not static. It's flexible and so are you. Timing is a key to some relationships being perfect and others not so much.

Step 4: Be Transparent.

This may sound like a cliche, but I've found being myself allows me to gain some instant connections with the type of people I'm looking to connect with.

You can't fake being a genuinely nice person. I need to give credit to the family I grew up in and the neighborhood where I grew up. Being one of 13 kids, having so many amazing family members, and living on the southside of Chicago taught me to build relationships with all ages when I was very young. I thought that was normal. Our neighborhood is great, because we have all economic levels, races, private, and public all in one location. By being myself, I am able to draw on those skills very naturally. I don't have to BS someone to find our shared points of connection.

A subset of this rule is: come from a place from giving first. The reason I put it as a subset is because I know a lot of people who approach people in an effort to connect, and they fake their goal of creating value for you first **but without transparency this all falls apart.**

Step 5: Know How To Ask

In all relationships, there will be a point where the person asks you: "What can I help you with?" or "How Can I Help You?" How you want to be positioned and perceived is vital—and you may only get one chance to answer.

Jocko Willink, Navy SEAL and author of *Extreme Ownership,* shares that when a senior officer would ask each guy in his unit if they need anything, Jocko's response was: "I'm good sir!"

Why? So that when he really needed something and he asked for it, his bosses knew he wasn't messing around. This is a great approach if you have an ongoing relationship with the other person, but what if you only get one chance to make an impression?

There are a few things you want to keep in mind:

- Everyone wants to help...the secret is you just need to make helping ridiculously easy.
- Ask in a way that creates zero pressure on the person you are contacting.
- Finally, if you are just there to extract value from others, then this system will be a waste of time for you.

Let's say you run into Mr. X, a powerful and well-connected world-class performer in your industry. The two of you strike up a conversation and are getting along fairly well. You know that this is your chance to make your ask, so you say:

"Do you mind if I ask you a question?"

"Not at all," Mr. X replies. "Fire away."

So you continue:

"I'm not sure if I'm even asking the right question, but I've been testing a lot of things. We spend over a million dollars a month in advertising a month, online and in newspapers, and a challenge we just ran into is ____."

(**Note:** I do this, because it shows I'm an action taker and shows humility. Most people don't lead with the mistakes they have made.)

Now, a supercharger in this opening is if you can share something that will make his eyebrows raise, because it makes him think: "Holy crap, this guy is doing something no one else is!"

Here's another example:

"I'm not sure if I'm even asking the right question, but I started my own business last year. My goal this year was to attend as many events on ABC. If you were in my shoes, what would be the first step you would take for mastering ABC at light speeds?"

Or:

"What question should I be asking you that I don't know enough to ask yet?"

That last one is awesome, because it gets anyone thinking. If they never have been asked it—which most people haven't—then you will see them go internal and search for the answer.

Stay silent and let them find it.

Step 6: Take Action At Superhuman Speeds.

If any of your dream contacts gives you advice or help, your #1 job is to take action as fast as humanly possible.

But there's a second step that is just as important: return to them with the results of their advice. NO ONE does this. It will instantly and forever leave an imprint on that person.

Step 7: Pay Them…

Many people are walking around expecting free stuff, but I gotta tell you that you start separating yourself by exchanging money with someone.

Here's a basic sequence that is available for most of us:

a. Buy their book.

b. Join a webinar or tele-call.

c. Attend a seminar or event they will be speaking.

i. This is great for many reasons

1. Meet like-minded people

2. See what they are like in person

3. Get a "feel" of the entire environment.

Then *and only then* should you hire them for a consulting gig or join their coaching program, unless you have the cash and you resonate at a high level.

The Final Step: There is one more way that you can provide value to your dream contacts and, in doing so, expand and enrich your Power Network. By being an expert or authority in an area that is 1) valuable to your contact and 2) outside of his or her own expertise. This can make you an indispensible contact and power relationship for them!

That brings us to the next phase of the Time Collapsing system: Creating Instant Authority!

Chapter 11:

INSTANT AUTHORITY SYSTEM

The biggest mistake I made in my 20's was thinking that just being "good" or "great" at something was going to make me successful. What you probably don't know is that I wrote a few really good books in my 20's, but had zero clue how to market and promote them.

Therefore Oprah and Ellen didn't come running to ask to have me on their shows.

The reality is if you want to get paid big dollars, get access to the VIP's, get your product, book, or podcast known by everyone, and have business chasing after you instead of the other way around, you need to understand how to position yourself as the ultimate authority in whatever you do.

The first key is realizing, assuming talent is equal or comparable, that Celebrity and Authority is **MANUFACTURED!**

Yep, I said it earlier and I'll say it again: **The game is rigged for those who understand it!**

There are ridiculously talented actors, singers, artists, and inventors working at a Starbucks during the day so they can do their thing for burgers at night, while people with their same (or even less) talent are famous, making all the money and getting all the fame.

Now, obviously that does not mean the more famous, more wealthy people aren't hustling and grinding. Frankly, that is assumed. The point is those people have figured out something that the non-earner hasn't!

No matter what business you are in, assuming you have a good product and you have the desire to work your butt off, **YOU ARE IN THE MARKETING AND PROMOTIONAL BUSINESS!** People who do this properly, regardless of the business, can charge superior fees, have people chasing them with checks in hand, and do whatever it is they want. Here's how you can create the same system for yourself.

1: Never Chase...Always Attract.

Whatever it is you think you want to go out and get—make it chase you. The most common myth when starting a business, podcast, or writing a book, becoming a singer, actor, ANYTHING is "get your name out there." The reality is that you want people chasing you because you give something away that creates enormous value. This value makes people come to your website, storefront, or calling your phone.

In our businesses we use marketing to get the "value offer" out to everyone, but ONLY highly qualified people show up at our door, store, and buy. This, in my experience, is the smartest, most powerful ways to go from ZERO to multiple 7- and even 8-figure sales a year very fast and with the least amount of risk and start-up capital.

2: Automate the Selling System.

These are personal preferences, but I only get into businesses that can run, market, and sell a product without my direct daily involvement.

If you ever think about opening something up locally that would require man hours and time in an office, you should ask: "Who is providing this value through the Internet?" With technology today, you can have people running your ads, driving them to your product page, a video, or a webinar 24 hours a day, 7 days a week.

Not only can you serve more people that way, but you will have built a business that gives you freedom. Shopify allows you to build an online store quickly. Amazon will allow you to sell just about anything up there and will fulfill your product. With Facebook, Pinterest, Instagram, and Google, you can target the people who are most likely to buy your products.

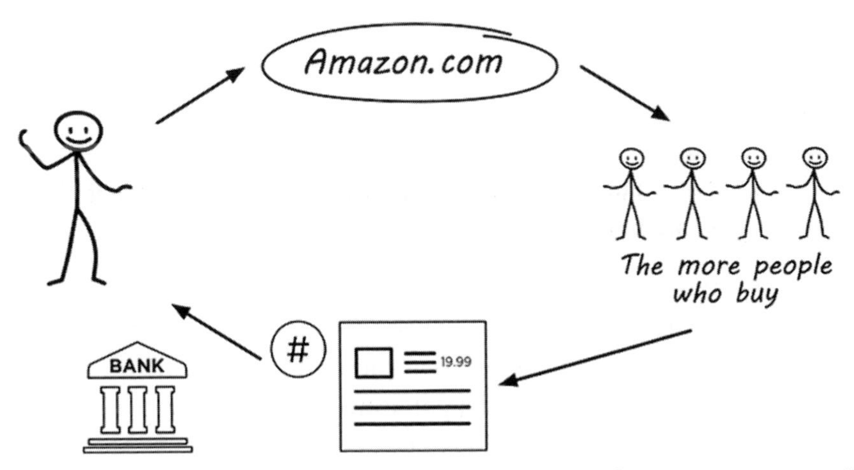

Many of my friends travel the world and work from remote areas all the time. This isn't something for the lucky few. It's something for people like yourself who have made a decision to be uncommon. For me, I get to be at my kids games or events at anytime and it NEVER affects sales. When we run our live events, it is always during the middle of the week so that weekends are completely free.

3: WHO IS SELLING TO THE HUNGRY CROWD?

Legendary copywriter Gary Halbert was famous for asking his audiences, **"What is the most important element in starting a new business?"**

No matter what people would say, the answer always came down to a "Starving Crowd." A group of people who desperately want their pain or frustration to go away, or for their passion to be catered to.

A secret component of leapfrogging to the top in business is understanding this concept, then identifying the **#1 player who is already serving in that crowd**. From there, you can go head to head with them or you can identify sub-markets or sub-niches you can divide and then lead.

The term "Riches in Niches" exists for good reason. My most profitable businesses had within them sub-niched out businesses that **drove the majority of the profits**. For example, when I ran a coaching business teaching dentists how to attract patients, I noticed a large majority of my clients wanted "implant" patients. By designing a catered product just for them, I was able to charge a lot more, because the value to them was very **specific, personalized, and had a higher payoff.**

In our health supplement business, one category that we started off with was "Longevity." By testing many different angles and approaches, we found that the "Heart market" really loved our supplements. By Sub-Niching the business, we found a goldmine. It also helped that we were one of the first businesses catering to that market.

Instead of going "broader" with your business, you may find going deeper to a more highly targeted customer will pay off with a LOT less overhead, headache, and competition.

Dollar Shave Club

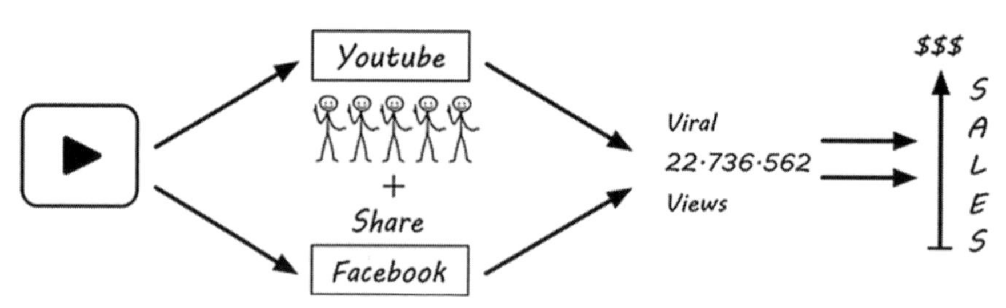

If your desire is to scale, go specific to then go broad. Learn from the following examples:

- Dollar Shave Club: They started by selling razors...now they are offering products for your entire bathroom.
- Amazon.com: Remember when they used to just sell books?... now they sell literally everything!
- Birchbox: They started off selling snacks...now they've expanded to selling wine.
- Zappos: Started with shoes...now they sell clothing for all ages.

These are just a few. Are you niched? Or are you broad? Either way, you can move up or down the ladder for more sales.

4: Create Your Rules of Engagement.

Every customer or client will want you to do things their way. If you become "everything to everyone," then you are nothing to no one. You will be treated in accordance with how you set up the relationship.

This pertains to employees, customers, subcontractors, third-party relationships, and much more. YOU need to put conscious thought and intention into your dream scenario and then build everything else around it.

This is TRUE LEAPFROGGING to the ideal life, because you are not waiting for certain circumstances that then allow you to set the terms of engagement. You do that at the beginning and everything flows from that perspective.

If you are a podcaster, artist, or author, being aware of your rights and who owns them is *very* important to think through on the "front-end"—meaning BEFORE you get shoulder deep in the trenches with someone who owns the rights to your information.The same is true with business relationships. In this case, defining your rules of engagement is absolutely essential to the health and longevity of making this a win-win for everyone involved.

5: POSITION YOURSELF AND/OR PRODUCT AS THE ULTIMATE AUTHORITY!

By putting yourself at the top, you can command higher fees for your service, charge higher prices for your product, and have people lining up to buy from you though proper educating of your prospect market. Every business can immediately increase their profits by doing any or all of the efforts below.

a. **Write a book, white paper, or special report:** In our society, people instantly put authors on a pedestal. If you are selling anything, you should have an educational process that helps people see the value in what you do.

   A book is the best business card you can have. With Amazon, you can write a short book and be live in a matter of a month if you are determined.

b. **Create a Video Training Series:** some people are excellent on video. You can take video from a seminar you have done or simply create one on your computer. You can then put leads or new customers through it. This is a process of "training the customer" so that they are educated, predisposed to buy from you, consume your service, and rave about you to others. An educated customer is 10X more valuable than an uneducated one.

c. **Get Interviewed On Podcasts, Youtube, or TV:** what do actors and actresses do when they are promoting their movies? They get interviewed!

Our culture has a built-in belief that states: if you are getting interviewed, you must be an expert. The funny thing is that ALL media is manufactured. Once you understand this, then you will understand that it's your JOB to make this process happen. There is no one going to come along and swoop you up to get your message out.

d. **Interview the Top Experts In Your Industry:** the same way getting interviewed positions you as the expert, when people see the quality of the people you have interviewed there is a co-branding element to it. You get associated with them and leapfrog to their level.

   The side benefit of doing this is you build a relationship with that individual and simultaneously are learning. If you follow-up properly by only focusing on creating value with these high level experts, you'll start seeing the boomerang effect of value coming your way.

e. **Speak On Stage:** If you are an expert, then let people know you are available to speak NOW. Authors and Mini-Celebrities are asked to speak at seminars. A close friend of mine who does over $1,500,000 net a year teaching people how to start a business online told me that his #1 customer acquisition strategy is being on stage.

f. **Hire Who You Want To Be Associated With To Be On YOUR stage.** Want to get connected and be associated with a Top Influencer? Want to pitch them an idea or do a product with them? Hire them to speak at your event. Put a mandatory lunch or meeting as part of the deal.

   Too expensive you might think? No problem! **Pass the bill on to your customers.**

   Let's say the speaker costs you $25,000. Your potential joint venture, business deal, or co-branding might be worth

$250,000 to you. Hold a seminar and charge $1,250-$10,000 per person. Then simply do the math:

If you charge $10,000, then you'll just need 3 people there to break even.

If you charge $1250, you'll need approximately 28, because you'll have other costs too.

One other hot tip: Identify other businesses that want access to your customers and charge them to be a sponsor at your event. Next thing you know, you aren't paying out of pocket for any of it.

g: **Licensing:** if something is already created, you can Time Collapse by paying a small licensing fee to have the rights to sell it. I've done this a few times and it allows me to see very quickly whether something is going to work or not. The cost of licensing can be just a simple "cost of goods sold."

Caution: there is more to this topic than I can cover in the book. The KEY is making sure you walk through all the numbers and scenarios to protect BOTH parties and ensure a WIN-WIN. If one party is not happy, then it's a losing scenario.

h: **Endorsements:** Nothing can add faster real world credibility to your name, product, or "thing", than a great endorsement. If you are looking to increase conversions and sales, ask yourself: "Who would my customers trust and believe?" The answer: other customers who are just like them.

Celebrity endorsements are great, because they cut through the clutter and get attention fast. **You can get someone who was an A-lister 15 years ago, and who is now a C-lister rather inexpensively.** However, the audience you are trying to reach will still PERCEIVE them as an A-list star! Giving you an amazing effect!

Last key question to ask yourself regarding endorsements: "Who is the center of influence in your space, whose endorsement would make all the dominos fall in perfect order?"

Once you have that answer, then you apply the Time Collapsing Power Relationship System!

Remember, no matter how good you are at something, if you don't have a plan of positioning yourself to create the perception you want, then you will not be able to utilize your knowledge, skill, credibility, and/or expertise at the level you'd like.

A less skilled, less credible, and non-expert can get more attention, more money, and more perceived authority simply by putting himself at the top!

Money, a Power Network, and instant authority can put you in the position to leapfrog to where you want to be. The next key is to STAY at the top. The next phase of the Time Collapsing system is going to show you how to learn from the best!

Chapter 12:

Modeling Greatness

Before Will Smith agreed to play The Greatest in the movie *Ali,* he said he just couldn't see "the Fresh Prince of Bel Air becoming Muhammad Ali."

That was until, Direct Michael Mann called. In an interview with Charlie Rose, Will explained that Mann had illustrated the curriculum for becoming Ali. He said:

"We are gonna eat what he ate. We are gonna run the distance that he ran. We are gonna train the way Muhammad Ali trained. We are gonna spar the way he sparred. Through the comprehension of the physical it will naturally bring you toward the mental/emotional space that a fighter lives in.

By understanding the mental and the physical, I will naturally understand the next phase—the spiritual, which is a necessity for understanding his strengths and convictions."

Smith took the advice to heart and modeled his life after the champion fighter. His performance was so convincing it earned him an Academy Award nomination.

If you're really looking to Time Collapse and reach the outcome you desire in the fastest way possible, modeling your behavior after someone who's already succeeded at creating your desired outcome is the fastest path between where you are and where you want to be.

The definition of modeling in this context is: to replicate a behavior, thinking pattern, and/or sequence of actions in order to replicate the same outcome.

The core belief you need to have in order to apply modeling to achieve accelerated results in your life is: ***"If someone else (person, business, team) is capable of doing it, so can I."***

By the end of this chapter you will...

- Be able to identify successful businesses, athletes, entrepreneurs, teachers, and/or other people of all walks of life that you'd like to replicate their results, and now apply a system for acquiring these skillsets and thinking patterns rapidly.
- Be able to create an unstoppable personal success system that applies to any field. The ability to identify, replicate, and execute new behaviors by choice can be applied anywhere by anyone.

We are already automatically modeling and applying this to our lives daily since birth, but most of us have zero idea that we are doing so. For example, why is it that most children end up mimicking the same things their parents or brother and sisters do?

They are simply replicating the behaviors they observe ... monkey see, monkey do. They see a consistent behavior. Then, ***without judgment or imposing their filters onto a situation or behavior***, they accept it and implement it into what they're doing.

We have actually already discussed a perfect example of what I'm talking about. Remember when my son, Mike, showed up for his first day of lacrosse camp and immediately began modeling after his coach's example? **What took careful observation at first became muscle memory after a few practices!**

We end up unconsciously building habits, behaviors, and lifestyles based on our worldview about what is right for us. Most likely this was passed down to us from those before us. This could be really good if you accumulated excellent behaviors or could be really bad if those you modeled are highly dysfunctional.

The good news is that by becoming aware of how to model behavior ON PURPOSE, you can wipe the slate clean and start building new, more supportive behaviors and thought patterns to get the outcomes you desire and benefit from most.

When you are in the education trap and "getting a job" trap, as discussed earlier, you end up being given your roles and responsibilities and are then shown exactly how to do things. Most people crave such "structure," however, this keeps them in the box that was set for them before they got there.

In the real world of success, you need to teach yourself most of what really works.

I have used modeling to learn pretty much every skillset I use in business today. Some of this was done by watching videos, going to seminars, hiring consultants one-on-one, or having someone show me something.

I used modeling as a core strategy for preparing for Mark Divine's Kokoro Camp. I found strategies for handling cold water, hiking for hours with a 30lb backpack; I installed the same belief systems that Mark Divine used when going through Hell Week in order to actually ***enjoy being in physically awful situations.***

My main operating question was: "What mental framework must he have had in order to enjoy such a physically uncomfortable and mentally challenging environment that few ever survive?"

He writes about these experiences in his books, *Unbeatable Mind: Forge Resiliency and Mental Toughness to Succeed at an Elite Level* and *The Way of the SEAL: Think Like an Elite Warrior to Lead and Succeed.*

Navy SEAL Hell Week loses approximately 80% of its enrollees. The people who pass aren't necessarily physically more superior, but they have an operating model of how they see the world, handle chaos, and a slew of other challenges differently.

The system works brilliantly.

When a high-level athlete called me for assistance because he was going through an extremely tough time dealing with injuries and performing at an elite level, the most important thing we did was use "self-modeling" to elicit his strategy for when he was at his best. From there, we worked to re-associate him to that strategy and feeling, then set him off in the right direction.

You can apply this chapter to yourself, right now, to get reassociated to the things you do very well and want to take to the next level and/or apply it to a person who has a skill you would like to acquire.

So, let's dive into how YOU can use modeling to attain ANY outcome you desire.

1: You Have to Be Intensely Interested About the Subject: Modeling begins with seeing, hearing, reading, or experiencing a glimpse of something that sparks INTENSE interest.

Most Mixed Martial Artists around my age seem to all say something like: "I fell in love with Brazilian Jiu Jitsu when I saw Royce Gracie, a smaller skinnier guy, absolutely destroy all these beasts at the first UFC!"

I first became curious about Neuro-Linguistic Programming when a man told me he could help people with past traumas without having to know any "content" about what had happened. I became insanely committed to HAVING to learn it when I saw Tony Robbins removing people's phobias[6] and eliminating emotional trauma on stage when I was 23 years old.

[6] **Snake Phobia Cure:** If you want to see a real world phobia cure done on live TV by the co-founder of NLP, watch Richard Bandler remove Michael Strahan's Snake Phobia: Click here: https://www.youtube.com/watch?v=w_xrTtjpCpE

When I heard someone from stage say: "Your income is directly related to your ability to write sales copy!" I was hooked! Game was on!

2: Let your Curiosity Lead You: When an experience sparks a curiosity and a series of thoughts like, "Hmm, I wonder if I could do that, or how can I do that?" take those thoughts one step further to: "I'd like to try that!" Or "I have to do this."

Step 3: Find Your Expert To Model!

Ask the Primary Question(s):

Who can teach me that? Where is a Master? Pro? Extraordinary Teacher?

Whose behavior can I replicate?

How do I get access to that type of information?

Who is the best in the world at it? Who is their coach?

These primary questions are powerful because, if you'll notice, they zoom straight to the highest level of expertise, performance, or instruction.

In my interview with Master Lloyd Irvin, which you can find at www.EdOKeefeShow.com, he shares how his first BJJ teacher went to Brazil, leaving him to fend for himself when it came to learning Brazilian Jiu Jitsu. In the absence of his coach, Irvin would study film of the highest level black belt competitions.

He was a brand new beginner but, because he is also a Time Collapser, he went right to the top and broke down film. He is one of only a handful of people who have received their black belts in Brazilian Jiu Jitsu in less than three years.

When I first started learning from him, he said something profound: **"Why do anything that is only going to work at the white belt level?**

Our goal is to win world championships at the black belt level so we only work on fundamentals that, when mastered, will work at that level."

Now is the time to ask yourself:

- Am I actively studying and modeling the best people with the skillset I want?
- Am I actively studying and modeling to make my desired outcome happen?"
- If the answer is "NO," then your next step is to ask:
- How can I put myself in the situation where I'm learning from the best in the world?

I have yet to come across any skillset or desired outcome that I couldn't attain by getting on an airplane and going to a seminar, hiring a consultant, or figuring out the steps of making my desired outcome happen. With YouTube, you can gain access to top notch training and teaching within seconds on virtually ANY topic in any field.

It's not magic that makes this possible; it's simply asking the right questions and modeling the right behaviors

When Steps 1, 2 and 3 are consistently followed the only possible outcome is a NEW REALITY in which anything is possible!

How I Used Modeling Steps 1, 2 and 3 to Make Money

In business, when I first learned that, "Your ability to make money is direct correlation to your ability to write sales copy..."

I accepted that statement at the time as 1000% fact. (Step 1)

I then said, "Okay, what is the process of learning writing sales copy ***at an accelerated rate?"*** (Step 2)

Notice the question asked assumes: ***"Accelerated rate."*** This is an INTENTIONAL assumption to collapse the timeframe it takes to create results. And in turn results come MUCH faster than people typically experience.

I then took ALL the steps that I described earlier:

I asked, "Who is the best in the world at copywriting?" Then, "What was their Core Strategy for learning copywriting quickest?"

The pattern that I noticed was that every top level writer said the same thing:

> *"If you want to become a great copywriter you need to write every single day.*
>
> *The best way to do it is to find the best copywriting letters, from the best copywriters of all time and hand write out every single bit of copy."*

So, without judgment, I did just that. **I accepted that strategy as 1000% truth.** I got up at 6:30 AM. Grabbed my cup of coffee, went to the Einstein Bagels, and hand wrote world-class sales letters and ads for 90 minutes every day. It was actually a pretty nice morning routine.

When you allow yourself to just go ahead and assimilate or integrate a new idea or behavior, rather than judging it, **your neurology picks up on it at a rapid pace.**

Now, the secret sauce for creating the right mindset for accelerated learning is doing it **without judgment and with a playful curiosity.** Every filter (the values, the belief systems, the sequences) that you would hope to acquire start naturally and unconsciously arising in your awareness, and start integrating into your neurology.

The reason I point this out is because most people try learning in an opposing fashion. They get stressed, they evaluate the instruction, skillset, belief system BEFORE ever trying it on. The brain works slower when it's being forced.

When you *allow* the patterns to integrate, rather than pushing them through, it become very easy to intuitively pick up on the filters of the high-performer you're modeling after.

Start with the precise physical movements or verbal rehearsing and you end up backtracking to the mental operating filters.

MODELING METHOD 1: THE PHYSICAL SHAPES THE MENTAL

In the opening of this chapter, I shared the story of how Will Smith gave an Oscar-nominated performance as Muhammed Ali by modeling the lifestyle and training habits of The Champ. This is the perfect illustration of how physical modeling shapes the mind. Smith was able to tap into Ali's mind because he was putting his body through the same work.

Will Smith's success in Ali is a great example of how physical modeling can build a framework the mental, emotional, and even spiritual model.

MODELING METHOD 2: THE MENTAL SHAPES THE PHYSICAL

The other approach is to start with the mental side of things and allow that to guide your internal strategy (thoughts, images, feelings) which then dictates your physical actions.

Once your physical actions are initiated, you then see what outcomes start showing up and make the necessary adjustments until you can replicate the outputs the person you're modeling already knows how to do.

If you don't have direct one-on-one access to the genius/expert you're modeling (99% of us don't) then you're going to do what I call, "virtual" modeling.

We have to imagine, project, or guess some of the sequences and steps required to create the BIG actions necessary for success. But any and all information we can gather about the processes of the person we're modeling will make it that much easier to replicate.

Questions To Ask When You Don't Have Direct One-on-One Access To The Expert/Genius You're Modeling

We start with a set of questions:

- What is the outcome that they are accomplishing that I want to replicate?
- How do they see the world? What is their Operating Model?
- Then we want to understand their "Filters To Greatness."
- How do they see themselves in the specific context? (Identity)
- What is important to them in this context? (values)
- What are the core drivers that motivate them? What are they moving away from? (pain) What are they moving towards? (pleasure/gain)
- What do they believe is possible? What do they think they are capable of achieving? (Beliefs)
- What skills do they have that enable them to do so? (Beliefs)

These questions give us the mental context that allows us to work the strategy and initiate the physical actions required. Without laying the foundation of this correct "mental context," you run the risk of applying a strategy in the wrong location.

Internal Strategy:

Now, let's move forward with understanding the internal strategy of the person you're modeling.

- When they begin to do (insert talent or emotional state), what is the first thing they do inside their mind, body, or heart?
- When do they know it's time to start? What specifically do they do to start?
- If they were going to teach you to do it, what would they ask you to do?
- How do they know when they are doing it at levels of excellence?
- What do they do when the results are not as expected, or they are not achieving the outcome they desire?

Our job is to put these steps in order and with as much specificity as possible. Ultimately our success is when we are getting the same outputs or better as they did.

If you do actually get to field questions at the person you're modeling, ask them these same ones! You may elicit their real core strategy, even that which had previously been done at an unconscious level. Because they aren't aware of these micro-distinctions, it may take a minute for them to answer some of these questions.

If the person says to you, "I don't know," simply say, "Don't worry about it, just make it up. What if you did know?"

You'd be amazed at how that opens them up and they answer the question. This not only expands the awareness of you (the student), but also the awareness of the expert as well (thus providing value to them). It's a win-win!

How Are YOU Going To Collapse Time With Modeling?

Let's start by identifying one or two people who are accomplishing or creating outputs that you'd like to replicate, so in turn you can model them.

- Who is making money you would like to make?
- Who is running a business that you would like to model?
- Who retired at a young age; what was their process?
- Who seems to have the ideal lifestyle that you'd like to experience?
- Who has the ideal body, energy, happiness that you would like to have?
- Who has the team environment that you would like to create in your house, company, or gym?

The applications are endless.
It's just a matter of you taking these Action Steps:

1. Identify Your Model (or Models).
2. Determine the Ideal Outcome That Would Need to Happen In Order For You To Know That You Have Successfully Modeled Their Strategy or Skill?
3. Build A Mental Model For How They See The World Within The SkillSet Context
4. Identify The Proper Sequences
5. Practice and Implement Skill-Set
6. Continue To Run Through A Feedback Loop Until You Optimize The Results

World renowned human behavior expert and author Richard Bandler has a simple process from his book *Guide to Trans-Formation!* that is a great help when you're modeling someone or something.

Try this:

1. Decide on a role model, someone whose physical performance you would like to replicate. Spend as much time as possible studying your role model in the flesh, on video or on TV. Simply relax while watching them, softening your vision and hearing and seeing the flow of the performance.
2. When you feel as familiar as possible with your role model's performance, close your eyes, relax and recreate your role models performing a sequence of actions at the highest level of excellence. See and hear everything there is to build a model of that competence.
3. When you have watched this performance for some time, move around the mental image of your role model and step inside. Imagine that you are able to see through the eyes of excellence, hear through the ears of excellence and feel the feelings of excellence.
4. Run through the same sequence of actions but from within, noticing this time what your body feels as you do this. Repeat several times as you have a sense of familiarity.
5. Step out of your role model's body, with the intention of retaining as much of the sill as possible as you return to normal working consciousness.
6. As soon as possible (and as much as possible) practice the borrowed skill, noticing how this exercise improves your performance.
7. Repeat the entire exercise, combining it with what-ever real time practice you do, at least once a day for the first 21 days, then at least once a week as maintenance

The Final Step: Modeling via study, observation, and research of the expert or high-performer you wish to emulate can take you a long way, BUT there is so much to be gained from one-on-one interpersonal relationships. If you can, I highly recommend using the Time Collapsing Power Network system to connect to those you are modeling after.

In the next chapter, we'll look at how mentor relationships can help you leapfrog ahead in expertise, authority, modeling, and building your network—and how, if you're not careful, mentorship can become a trap.

Chapter 13:

THE MENTOR SYSTEM

Think about this: there are people out in the world who have spent 10, 20, or even 50 years or more doing the thing you want to accomplish.

No amount of super-learning or speed strategies can beat tapping into the knowledge of those who have built up that much wisdom over time. That is why finding a great mentor is absolutely critical for your journey.

WHAT IS THE DIFFERENCE BETWEEN MODELS AND MENTORS?

A Model (which we've talked about) is a person or business system whose success you want to emulate, duplicate, innovate from, and accelerate beyond. I recommend only have one or two models at a time to avoid confusion and mixing parts.

Mentors, on the other hand, will help guide you through the process, offering advice, support, resources, and most importantly offer key distinctions. The most useful thing they do is to help you not make the mistakes you would otherwise make, and make it easier to face obstacles.

HOW DO YOU DECIDE WHAT TYPE OF MENTOR YOU NEED?

Your critical aim will determine who you seek out for mentorship. You want to have people who have specialized knowledge about the gaps you are going to need to fill, but who also have a broad experience base.

A mentor can help you with everything from getting started, getting your first sale, taking your product or idea to multiple channels, raising capital, scaling, and/or selling a company. While there are always crossover skills from one business to another, the depth of knowledge required to excel fast in a certain industry is even more important.

In my health supplement business, I hired a direct mail professional who had over 10 years experience in THAT industry. We worked with a list manager (Macromark) who specialized in THAT industry.

If I wanted to learn the best system for doing Facebook marketing, solo email ads, and Google display networks, for example, I would find others who spend 90-100% of their time DOING THAT. Specialization is really important when it comes to selecting the right mentor for what you want to do.

HOW DO YOU FIND THE MENTORS WHO WILL SUPPORT AND COACH YOU?

First, the best mentor is a person that is 100% unconditionally available and ready to support you.

This is rare, but it is possible.

The more likely best mentors to find are in books, audio trainings, and on YouTube. Whenever I want to learn more about a particular subject, I go straight to YouTube to find a neverending list of experts who are sharing their expertise.

VIRTUAL MENTORS ARE AVAILABLE FOR FREE!

Podcasts are absolutely FREE and have a wealth of phenomenal information that literally can shape your mind. From Tim Ferriss, Spartan Up, SEALFit, and Lewis Howes, who are consistently putting out useful and inspirational content, to seeking out specific guests wherever they appear—I recently listened to Stephen Pressfield (author of *War of Art, Do The Work,* and *Gates of Hell*) on Joe Rogan's podcast, and it was amazing—there is so much amazing content out there just waiting to be downloaded..

I pretend that I'm just hanging out and am part of the conversation! Make sure you join me over at my "Ed O'Keefe Show Podcast," too.

CreativeLive is another fast-growing platform where, for a small fee, you can get access to trainings from people who are *killing it* in their field.

ATTEND LIVE EVENTS AND SEMINARS

A lot of potential mentors are running seminars, live events, or holding masterminds. Go there! No level of virtual training can replicate being fully immersed in a LIVE training environment.

At our Time Collapsing Academy events, people have massive breakthroughs from side conversations, million dollar deals happen, and literally ANY resource you need can be found in the room among attendees!

It's that simple. Being an entrepreneur can feel like you are in no man's land and that no one understands you. You need to go where people like you and where you want to be are hanging out. The best thinkers and learners attend those events because that is where they get the jet fuel to skyrocket their ships in many cases.

PERSONAL CONSULTING/COACHING

Hiring a personal consultant or coach can compress those time frames even further.

The reason this is so effective is you are compressing years of wisdom. This is one layer deeper of intensity than when you attend someone's seminar, or mastermind. It's very difficult to get the "expert" to spend time and get the entire picture on your individual plan in those environments. It's much better, in my opinion, to hire someone.

I use consultants to constantly gain specialized insight, help clarify my thinking, and get me brought up to speed for "what's working now" in particular industries. Investing the money to get them to focus solely on you, your goals, and your business is worth it.

Your key responsibility is to have clarity on what you want to accomplish when hiring a consultant. What are the possible outcomes for which you need assistance?

Depending on what you need, you might get a LOT of content and insight. OR, if you are in a more mature phase, you may be simply looking for a distinction here or there.

Either way, it's INVALUABLE...provided you're working with the right person.

Last, if a consultant can help you avoid mistakes you can't see and save you months, years, or even a decade of time, their value in this case may appear very subtle; however they have done an extraordinary service for you because they've saved you TIME, making this choice a VERY wise investment.

THE INFORMAL MENTOR

Some of the best life-long mentor relationships stem from connection or created value..mostly on your part for them.

If you want to have someone mentor you, find out how you can create value for them first. There are so many takers out there... and you don't want to be "that guy."

Do your research before meeting a potential mentor for the first time, learning everything about them and their story. If there are updated blogs, videos, podcasts, or trainings, stay plugged in. I've noticed a lot of podcasters will share what they are working on often when interviewing guests. If you can create value for an upcoming project your desired mentor is working on—then go to extremes to do so.

When you have your chance to meet them, you'll have insight that most don't; and I suggest that you ask questions that nobody else has asked them, which simultaneously positions you as a "humble hustler."

Here's a quick example:

> "You know, I've been doing this for X number of years and had __________ success, but made _________ mistake. If you were in my shoes, how would you have handled this problem?"
>
> "We just went to market with our new product. Our average cost per sale is $100, but the problem we are having is that our average sale is $120. We're actually losing $20 every sale when factoring all costs. When you guys grew (Insert their company) were you ever in this situation? If so, what was your key focus in order to break through?"

Another way of segueing into a question is:

> "I'm not even sure what to ask you, but based on [my situation] what should I be asking or thinking about in order to (insert goal you want to achieve or what you want to avoid)?"

When you share this, you're likely to get one of the following responses:

- Their response will reveal that they don't know what they're talking about—and that allows you to move on despite potentially being disappointed.
- "That's a great question, but I need more time to answer it. In order to help you, you should set up a day of consulting." Coaching is fine, but in many cases the immediate sell is a red flag. Do an energy check, and realize that being open will attract the best mentors but also attract sharks.
- They give you a good targeted slew of questions and/or answers. If they are really good, it will be both.

The reason I like the sequence of reading a book, listening to a podcast, or watching a video, then going to a seminar, then coaching, or consulting is that it gives me multiple opportunities on the front side to evaluate them.

CONGRUENCY CHECK

Time and multiple interactions allows you to see if a potential mentor's attitude and actions are truly congruent to their teachings. While no one is perfect, and students can unrealistically put people on pedestals. You want to make sure you are aligned with this person too. At the very least, you have the awareness of their personality and behavior that might not match yours, and you determine whether or not that's cool with you.

THE BEST ADVICE I CAN GIVE THAT WILL SEPARATE YOU FROM EVERYONE ELSE!

If you're taking action, learning a lot, attending seminars, coaching clubs, and hustling you will start attracting people in your life who could potentially mentor you. Once you've found a mentor that you click with, here are a couple things you'll want to keep in mind:

- Be completely transparent and honest (you'll filter out the people who aren't there to support you and attract the opposite).
- There needs to be an agreement (even a nonverbal one) to be completely honest with each other, so you can share your worst mistakes and they can give you honest feedback, both without judgment.
    - To start building this trust, be blunt and vulnerable and start sharing your mistakes (if they judge you or have no feedback to offer, get out of the mentor relationship!)
    - Also, keep your cool and thank them for feedback when it stings, and then take action immediately and come back to them with results.

Last, be patient! While this book is about speed, who you trust, and advice you act upon will have years of impact in your life.

What works for a successful person might be different for you. Trust yourself! Overtime, you will be building your own system that will look and feel perfect for you!

Chapter 14:

KNOW THE LANDSCAPE, KNOW THE RULES, KNOW THE LIES YOU TELL YOURSELF

Up to this point, a lot of the work we've been doing in building out your Time Collapsing system has been focused on your internal world—your filters, belief systems, friction points—and the actions you can take on your to leapfrog ahead to wherever you want to be. The final piece of the puzzle is to look at your environment to answer a few key questions:

1. What is the landscape I'm playing in?

2. What are the rules?

3. What are the lies I tell myself? What lies do other people tell each other?

This is critical, because it directly affects how you apply the Leapfrog Theory, which mentors you choose to seek out, and the individuals, organizations or teams that you plan on modeling. It determines the specialized knowledge you are going to acquire, the team you will build, and the time, effort, energy, money you plan on investing into all of it.

Most will ignore this principle, because it actually tells you to slow down and get grounded, determine what you are playing, discern what everyone else has verbally or nonverbally come to some agreement on—and then decide how you will change the rules, rewrite the gameplan, bend reality, and leap to the top at record speed.

Listen closely as I say this:

99% of the stuff you see that seems successful...is not.

99% of the stuff people say is working... no longer does.

If it does work...it won't for long.

The top 3% are rarely sharing their stuff in public... so you MUST GO DEEP with this principle.

So when it comes to understanding the landscape, the rules, and the lies you tell yourself, these key questions are cutting through to a key thread: the context. If you can't answer the three questions I listed above, it's a safe bet that you don't fully understand the context you're entering. And whether or not you honestly understand the context will determine whether you're set up for success, failure, heartbreak, or some combination of the three; so once you think you've grasped each component, ask whether those things are true and whether they're prone to change anytime soon.

Here are some examples:

Let's take Lance Armstrong's seven Tour De France wins—and how those titles came to be stripped.

The Landscape: EVERYONE IS DOPING.

The Rules (in this case a non-verbal agreement among athletes)**:** If everyone is doping...it's okay to dope. NONE of us will talk about it.

Lies they tell themselves: I must dope to compete at the highest level for the sport.

In Armstrong's case, the landscape and the lie stayed consistent; the rule changed. Other cyclists started talking about the doping. Now, could Armstrong have won his titles if he started racing clean in a field that was still pretty dirty? Who can say? But if he had recognized that changing rules and adjusted accordingly, his career might have been spared the deathblow.

When I launched my Health Supplement Business, I wanted to ramp up to mailing 1,000,000 pieces a month because I had heard other marketers who had scaled and sold their business did this.

The Rule: Successful marketers mail 1,000,000 pieces a month.

The lie I told myself: If I'm going to compete, I need to mail 1,000,000 pieces a month.

While we got up to mailing 800,000 pieces in a month, what the "experts"/mentors whom I was hiring failed to share with me was how much capital I really needed to make this possible and profitable.

The other thing I failed to notice was: **The Landscape had changed!**

There simply weren't as many health supplement buyers that had been previously available for the other companies. Secondly, the internet was emerging and most of the buyers that were coming off my mailings didn't have email addresses.

While direct mail is STILL a good medium from which you can grow a very healthy business, you need to know new rules of engagement. The same applies for every media out there. They all work, it's a matter of knowing the REAL landscape, the real rules, and not succumbing to the lies.

When I moved the business primarily online, I assumed I would need 8 products going out to the market in order to hit $10,000,000/year. However, when one product took off, we actually did over $20,000,000 in one year.

I hadn't realized the power of one good compelling offer that people are happy to buy. The amount of traffic (or people) available on the internet. And how you can take that one offer and grow it so much, so fast.

Then the landscape changed again: in the past few years alone, the percentage of people who are visiting our website has gone from 80% desktop and 20% mobile just a few years ago to now more than 50% are visiting from a mobile device. This means that businesses HAVE to be built around this emergence of mobile. That's a rule.

When I started my dental marketing business in 2003-2004, we placed lead generation ads in trade magazines. While it was a success, it was nothing compared to the success the "experts" told me to expect.

Why? One main reason was that it was costing me around $40-$100 to acquire a lead, however, when they started their business in a similar market it was costing just $2-$4 per lead. The economics of the business had changed due to timing, competition, saturation, decreasing readership, and competitors running similar ads.

Landscape change was used to our benefit as well, because the internet allowed us to start getting leads at a cheaper rate while offline leads were increasing. If you can correctly assess the changing landscape, you will be setting yourself up to capitalize on it. The ability to get in the game and make a phenomenal impact is available *anyone* who takes action—and we're already seeing that in all the amazing disruption, creativity, and output happening across industries.

Changing the Landscape, Rules, and Lies

In Salim Islam's book, *Exponential Organizations,* he lists out the ex-ternal and internal transformations that are literally changing the way business is run while making 10X impact! Th ese are the changes to the landscape and the rules that could make the lies business owners or CEO's currently tell themselves very costly.

Staff on Demand: you can tap into a vast worldwide network of talent anytime you need it. Today, you can hire your designers from 99Designs, programming from Rent-A-Coder or Upwork—all as you need them. Fiverr.com has experts from all over the world who can do pretty much anything you need online.

Community and Crowd: By building your own tribe, you can simply tweet or post a request to your network and the answers and resources are there ready to help you.

Algorithms: Machine-learning can solve problems, build things, and do jobs at light speed.

Leveraged Assets: Own only what is critical to your business and outsource the rest. Companies that build their business by owning all their own assets can lose their flexibility. If someone else has a core competency better than yours and it's not within your aligned plan, hire them, but don't try and replicate it.

Gamification: Use gamification to motivate the right behaviors for business, sales, education, and referrals. That which is rewarded is repeated, right? It's the same reason my kids love playing on apps that give them badges for getting to the next level. Gamification is being used to incentivize students, employees, and customers.

Then there are the **Internal** developments, the things within our technology that are revolutionizing the way business is done and companies are ran.

Interfaces: Use them to make communication easy. Tools like Basecamp, Skype, GoToMeeting, and Slack are changing how teams communicate. There is almost no reason at all to travel for a face-to-face meeting.

Dashboards: Track data obsessively so you can make better decisions.

Experimentation: Create small experiments to keep what might work and what doesn't.

Autonomy: Allow your employee to have space to do their best work. This comes with a caveat though: you need to hire employees who will thrive in this ever-changing environment.

Social Technologies: Use them to coordinate and communicate with your teams.

Not only is the evolving landscape changing the way we work, it is also changing the marketplace. The technologies listed below are disrupting entire industries by becoming more affordable. As these amazing tools become more accessible, the landscape will be primed to change once again and the "old" rules will no longer apply!

3D Printing: build cars, jewelry, lawn mowers and just about anything from a simple program.

Industrial Robots: what had cost $500,000 dropped to under $22,000 in less than 5 years.

Drones: dropped in Cost from $100,000 in 2007 to $70,000 to $1,000.

Solar Energy: decreased in cost by over 200X in past 30 years.

3D Sensors: decreased in price by over 250X in past 5 years.

Neurotech: decreased in pricing 44X in past 5 years

Nanotech: projected to decrease in pricing by over 80% by 2020.

DNA Sequencing: $100,000,000 to $1,000! That is over a 10,000X decrease in pricing in 7 years.

These breakthroughs in the landscape, social media, and technology are allowing companies to reinvent markets. And then there's another huge landscape change that we need to discuss: the huge change to our GLOBAL economy that's just on the horizon.

GLOBALIZATION AND THE RISING BILLION

The most dramatic (positive) change in our global economy is about to occur between 2016 and 2020.

Three to 5 billion new consumers, who have never purchased anything, never uploaded anything and never invented and sold anything, are about to come online and provide a mega-surge to the global economy,[7] says Peter Diamandis, the CEO of XPRISE.

Consumers from all over the world now can access your product directly through your website or a site like amazon. And a BILLION more will be coming over the course of the next few years! A way to capitalize on this is to take something that is selling like crazy in the United States and be a "first mover" by bringing it to other countries. The competition will be less in most markets, which will give you tons of **distinction.**

I bring all of this up to show you just how quickly things are evolving and changing—and how much more is likely to change in a very short amount of time. As you can see, the landscape is changing rapidly and so are the rules. The lies people tell themselves will always be there, but with these new skills and awarenesses you can challenge assumptions and see what no one else is seeing.

And for Time-Collapsers this means opportunity!

---

[7] Diamandis, Peter. "The 'Rising Billion' New Consumers Will Arrive by 2020." The Huffington Post. June 06, 2015. Accessed June 29, 2016. http://www.huffingtonpost.com/peter-diamandis/rising-billion-consumers_b_7008160.html.

ACTION PLAN:

What is Your Landscape?

- What are the rules of the landscape you are planning to attack?
- Who are the leaders?
- Who is dictating the rules?
- What is the biggest threat inside this landscape?
- What is the biggest opportunity within this landscape?

What are the current rules (verbally or non-verbally agreed upon by the **businesses** in the market place)? What is the opposite or counter-example of this "rule"?

	Current Rules	**Counter-Example? Opposite?**
1.	____________________	____________________
2.	____________________	____________________

What are the current rules (verbally or non-verbally) agreed upon by the **customers** in the market place?

	Current Rules Counter	**Example? Opposite?**
3.	____________________	____________________
4.	____________________	____________________

How can you challenge your assumptions?

And, finally, do any of those rules *have* to apply to you? No, I'm serious! Is it possible that the lie you're telling yourself is that you have to play according to the "rules"? After all, you already know how to bend reality, time and space to put it into your service—why shouldn't you change the rules while you're at it?

Chapter 15:

The Time Collapsing System in Action!

Have you heard of the man *Forbes* calls "The Mad Billionaire"? If you don't know Nick Woodman by name, you'll certainly recognize the product that leapfrogged him to the top of his industry.

Feeling burned after his first start up failed, Nick Woodman was living the beach bum life out in Indonesia and Australia. He and his buddies were out surfing world-class waves, and Nick wanted to capture some action shots of them out on the water. His options were pretty limited—a disposable camera in a waterproof case—but Nick made it work with a contraption he wrangled out of rubber bands and a busted surfboard leash. It was his first prototype.

His wrist strap worked great and allowed Nick to maneuver the camera around to catch the shot he wanted, but the camera wasn't holding up its end. One wipeout and—boom—the case was flooded, or even busted apart. Nick realized he needed a camera that could withstand water, getting tossed around, and maybe even a drop or two and still take great photos. As he says it, "I realized I shouldn't be a strap company, but a camera company."[8]

---

[8] Moritz, Robert. "Guts, Glory, and Megapixels: The Story of GoPro." *Popular Mechanics*. N.p., 12 June 2012. Web. 18 June 2016.

The rest is history. GoPro sales have more than doubled every year since the first camera's debut in 2004. In 2012 the company sold 2.3 million cameras and grossed $521 million, according to Woodman; with $100 million in sales in January alone, that annual figure should again double this year.

Woodman's strategy: He "scratched his own itch" and turned his passion into a billion dollar business. This is the same approach Jesse Itzler took with Marquis Jets. In Itzler's own words, "Worse case scenario is that we get to fly privately, then it's a win!"

Nick Woodman didn't stew in his startup failure (at least, not for too long). He had a directional pull that was moving him forward...and he followed it.

Whatever influences you and wherever you're starting—whether you're scratching an itch, leading with passion, driven by frustration, ignited by your superpower, or following your desire to solve a problem—follow it!

CREATING YOUR PERSONAL TIME COLLAPSING SYSTEM!

My goal with this book is that you will be able to take these tools, and build out your own Time Collapsing System so that you can predictably create Time Collapsing Moments that will build to your Tsunami of Success!

That moment when all the momentum from your past effort combines with your current talent and strategies, and synergistically meets with other forces and timing to create exponential results beyond what you could have imagined!

This chapter's goal is to start pulling all the tools, ideas, concepts together for you in a simple way, so you can create your own Time

Collapsing System. Let's break down one of my big Time Collapsing moments so you can see the system at work.

Building My Health Supplement Business (For the Second Time)

My first attempt going into this category of business online was a disaster filled with lessons. I give away an 80-page report detailing out all the lessons at EdOKeefeShow.com so I'll pass over the first failed attempt and jump into my second attempt.

Step #1: I chose the Health Supplement Business. My criteria for this decision: I wanted a market that I could sell a product that I believed in. One that people would consume and repurchase. A business that wasn't based around my name and personality like my dental marketing business had been.

Understanding your criteria for doing "X" is vital, because each business will have it's pros and cons; but if you are aware of "WHY" you chose it, you will be aware of most of these things as they show up. You can mitigate much of the angst!

Step #2: I Chose the Media To Test. I opted to use direct mail because it was an old, long-term market with sustainability.

Step #3: I hired my consultant who built my team! I hired a woman who kicked ass at her job and I knew she fully internalized where I was wanting to go. So when she went out and got the doctor and the copywriter, I knew I could trust her choices. After meeting them I extended my trust to them too. I knew they didn't need me checking in or micromanaging, and that freed me up for other things! When they came to me with all the market research behind the supplements ready to go, all I had to do was to select the high quality products I wanted to sell, with the full assurance that they were in line with what I wanted.

Step #4: Credibility: The doctor on our team was one of the leading doctors in longevity. Not only could I implicitly trust the recommendations he made, but his reputation also boosted that of our brand. (Can you already see how we're leapfrogging?)

Step #5: Test Fast And Scale: Then we launched with a 60,000 direct mail piece test. Quickly we were mailing 120,000, and then 300,000, and eventually 800,000 pieces.

The problem, I quickly realized, was that I was under-capitalized and cash poor.

Step #6: Test Other Medias: this led me to going online and testing with direct email buys, also known as solo ads. To my surprise, I was profitable within 5 days on some of my tests. This was a completely different experience than what I was finding in direct mail. (I realized the landscape was changing!)

Even though my revenue was lower, my cash flow was better. Profit was better. I wasn't going to run out of potential places to advertise and people to mail, which was definitely going to be a challenge in direct mail.

Step #7: Keep Testing, Testing, Testing: Even though things were better, it took me close to one year until things "popped" and cash flow quickly flowed into my bank rather than out of it. I wrote about this in the Preface of the book.

Step #8: Add More Products To Sell Your Existing Customers: this is basic math. Research shows that your existing customers will be 16X more profitable than going out and acquiring new customers. Here are three solid "tricks" of the trade to getting data on what they might buy BEFORE ever spending money on creating your own product.

a. **Sell advertising space to your existing customers.** You'll be able to see what gets the the most opens and clicks if in email. If you rent your names to direct mail and/or email, when a person buys more advertising from you, that's a CLEAR indicator that their product is profitable. You can simply go create your own version of it.

B. **Sell other people's products as an affiliate.** You'll know based on your commissions whether or not it was profitable.

c. **Find complementary products from EBAY or Amazon, host it in your store and promote it to a small segment of your customers.** If people buy it, then simply buy it off amazon or ebay and ship it to them. Now that you know a small segment will buy, it's likely it will sell well to the rest of your customers.

Step #9: Leverage Other Platforms or Distribution Channels: Right now, a third of our sales come from Amazon.com. I love it and we are investing a lot of time and energy expanding this channel. Why? Because Amazon is growing by leaps and bounds and a business that has quality products and can get good reviews has a great opportunity to ride the wave with them.

So there you have it—that was my Time Collapsing structure while building out my healthcare supplement business. While I gave more detail than I originally planned, the REAL purpose of this chapter is to give you the bigger "structure" and sequence where possible. My hope is that in reading how one of my Time Collapsing moments came to be your mind is racing with ideas about what YOUR system might look like!

Because the thing is I can't tell you what yours will look like. There's no step-by-step, "do this, now do that" guide to Time Collapsing. Your process will be uniquely your own—and structures of each of your Time Collapsing moments will probably be unique too!

Last thought: this Time Collapsing System is no longer a book, but a process that you own. It is YOURS.

It's hard to give you EVERYTHING you need in a book, however, you now DO have a framework that gives you a serious LEAP compared to 99% of the people out there.

The world is waiting for you to go make something awesome!

Want more training? Head over to edokeefeshow.com and TimeCollapsingAcademy.com for a TON of free advanced training.

Now that you've learned the Time Collapsing process and seen all of the different ways and directions you can put it to work for you, let's move on to discuss what you'll need to know while you're in the midst of your own process.

The next section will talk about the tools, ideas, and beliefs that will help you sustain the success you attain through Time Collapsing. We'll discuss the mental toughness you'll need to pull yourself through difficult or frustrating moments; the soft side of success and the importance of kindness. We'll talk about the paradox of success, and how to stay above the fray. Finally we'll talk about how to determine what "wealth" and "success" really look like to you, and I'll show you an incredibly effective way to get your top priorities straight.

PART III:

Meaning

Chapter 16:

The Invisible Face of Mental Toughness

The face of mental toughness has usually been taken on by an athlete late in an excruciating game or match that pulls off a victory in spite of all odds.

Michael Jordan scored 38 points and had seven rebounds, five assists, and three steals in the 1997 conference finals despite the fact that he was so wracked with flu he needed to be carried off the court by Scottie Pippen. His performance has been attributed to his mental toughness and an absolute refusal to lose.

Of course, mental toughness happens outside of the sports world as well. We see it in the excellence of our soldiers as they withstand even the most extreme circumstances: cold, heat, and being asked to do hard work for long periods of time day after day. That takes serious mental toughness.

And when it comes to the entrepreneurial world? Don't even get me started.

Each person's crucible—no matter what sphere it's in—can not only forge them into a "tougher" person, but also simultaneously reveal to oneself a side that is normally buried. ***A more primal self, capable of doing***

things they never thought possible, battling back external forces, and literally having to renegotiate with reality in order to make themselves compete, endur, or forge ahead.

Sadly, many of the problems that our society faces today are a byproduct of having a poor understanding of the mind, body, and spirit's true potential. The symptoms show up as lack of ownership, lack of commitment, self-doubt, and a need to constantly judge others.

The physical manifestation of this shows up in obesity, poor self-control, self-destruction, sabotage in the face of success or opportunity, and passive aggressiveness towards other people...just to name a few.

These are all items that reflect a poor use of the mind's potential and lack of understanding of what you are capable of accomplishing. **The fact is none of us really know what our limits are until we step up to their borders.**

You can be surrounded by teammates, coaches, friends, colleagues, or business partners, but ultimately this meeting has to happen on a one-on-one level with yourself.

In the book: *Hard Things About Hard Things*, successful Venture Capitalist Ben Horowitz states:

"People always ask me, "What's the secret to being a successful CEO?' Sadly, there is no secret, but if there is one skill that stands out, it's the **ability to focus and make the best move when there are no good moves.** It's the moments where you feel most like hiding or dying that you can make the biggest difference as a CEO."

I remember a time when I was working out in my backyard on a nice late spring day. Our business was growing, cash flow was finally moving in the right direction, we were about to make the turn. A hole in our company was that our fulfillment center, who also acted as our call center, kept dropping the ball.

I decided to give them 30 days notice that we were moving our center over to a more reliable one. What I didn't know was that there were a handful of other clients doing the same thing...all at the same time.

The call center decided to simply shut their business down. Turn off the phones. Stop responding to customers. And plan to go bankrupt.

Their plan became a huge problem for us because we had made a crucial mistake: we allowed them to control our phone number. What this meant was that when customers were calling to find out where their order was all they would hear was a curt message: "This phone number has been disconnected."

Thousands of customers were not getting our product and when they called, they heard the message above. They panicked (rightfully so) and that led to a TON of refunds and chargebacks. In a matter of days we went from being on the right path to being on the edge of a cliff!

I remember taking a walk around the block right after it happened, and all I kept saying to myself was: "I always find a way. This situation will only force me to become a better entrepreneur. Where others might quit, I get stronger."

As I write this, I don't know if I ever shared with my wife how close I came to losing the entire company. I had a small group of great entrepreneurs who I was able to reach out to get their insights. Their help was vital, but ultimately I was on my own.

Sometimes even my brain was working against me. It would insert thoughts into the middle of my day that were FAR from helpful:

I can't do this....

I'm in pain, exhausted, tired, weak...

Those thoughts made it even more difficult to feel like I was in a position to take back control. I'm sure you've found yourself in a similar position before too. So, the most important question is: Can we develop mental toughness if we feel like we are mentally weak?

Answer: YES!

Forging Mental Toughness Through The Physical

It's easy to re-find your mental toughness when you get physical, because the body will let you know immediately that you are pushing outside of its limits. The voices of doubt, weakness, and/or self-preservation will kick in, attempting to "protect" you by moving you back to the status quo.

With rare exception, the discomfort and voices are just illusions. We all have them. They pop up even when you are baddest person on the planet and in the weirdest ways. I see doing something that is physically difficult as a way of purposefully calling those voices out. Seriously, call them forward! And then do two more laps or five more push-ups just to show your body and your brain that, **even though it may feel uncomfortable, you are in control**.

Your job is to create a new internal voice that has a much deeper belief of what is possible. Looking at the weak voices and internally laughing at them because seeing them for what they are dissipates their power. It shrinks them down and lowers their volume until it overrides them.

Use Contrast And Perspective To Your Favor!

Someone else always has it worse than you. It may not feel that way, but even if you are at the lowest of lows, you can "bend" your reality as we discussed earlier to borrow the mindsets of people who have overcome what you are currently experiencing.

Find 3-5 people in your life whom you would say are the toughest people you know, and borrow their mindset.

My good friend, Sean Stephenson, is one of the most positive people I've ever met. Yet, if anyone had a good reason to be miserable Sean was that guy.

He was born with a rare bone disorder that made his bones extremely fragile and stunted his growth. His parents were told that he wouldn't last 24 hours. Now, 35 years later, Sean is still alive and as he puts it, "all those doctors are dead."

Sean has two core beliefs. #1: Never believe a prediction about the future that doesn't empower you; and #2: believe that everyone is rooting for you to win even if they don't know it.

His message is simple: don't pity yourself and don't bully yourself. And if that's his mindset in the face of the physical setbacks he deals with everyday, then we have no excuse for pouting over a delayed launch.

Forging Mental Toughness Through The Spiritual!

Many people find their "strength" through their spirituality or religion. Having a belief that all things are happening to either teach a lesson, give me strength, provide me with an opportunity to grow is a good thing! My life has been enormously helped—and my mental toughness has been fortified—by the positive belief systems and guiding principles of my faith.

Staying Present + Positivity Works

When it comes to the teams I've coached, I've always noticed that a three-day national tournament FEELS heavy. Three days of all-out competition feels like a large task in the present moment. However, I offer my players the following advice to keep their heads in a calm, productive, and mentally tough state:

Focus on staying in the here and now. Control what you can control and the "pressure" won't get away from you.

Chunk the goal into micro-goals:

a. Tonight we will get a good meal. Get hydrated...THEN
b. Team Meeting to review our morning pre-game and our first opponent only.
c. Early morning wake, eat/hydrate and get to gym. Get to our court early. THEN...
d. Win the Warm-Up. Show good ball control, work up a good sweat...THEN...
e. Make the first pass an aggressive one.

If I can get a team to execute on this plan, then everything starts falling into place. The tournament isn't "hard" when there are only one or two things to focus on at a given time.

If you think of a goal, project, or challenge you are facing and you move the entire thing to *now*...it feels hard, correct?

But, if you stop and take a deep breath, and say something positive like: "I've Got This! This makes me stronger!" you'll calm yourself down. From there, expand the project like an accordion out into a longer timeline in which you can see each step broken up into smaller pieces.

Now you've just got one small step in front of you. Easy, right? By using micro-goals and chunking big things into small pieces, you gain control of something massive and make it achievable.

GOING TO THAT DARK PLACE!

If you watch the Crossfit Games, you'll hear the announcers say something like: the athlete is "going to have to go to their Dark Place" or "Pain Cave." The line is so common that it's actually more of compliment when you're throwing it around the gym. It recognizes that the athlete knows how to dig in, grit their teeth, and find the energy to finish the work.

The presupposition is that some people have the capability to do this and others don't. I disagree. I think we all have the capacity to find our deep strength when we need it. Is it possible that this "dark place" needs to be prepared and trained the same way you train in the gym? Yes, I believe so.

A great way to do this is to create a place in your mind that you have prepared for these type of situations. Then utilize it when you are training, meditating, or in the middle of extraordinarily tough times. Following one of Mark Divine's meditations for creating your own Mind Gym. I created a place that is in the woods. Surrounded by amazing trees and fall colored leaves.

There is a stone place to sit or stand in front of depending on what is going on. Behind me and to the sides, I am surrounded by animals that all mean something to me.

To my right sitting is a lion. To me it is my symbol of power, strength, and calming protection. Being a father of 7 children, I feel like a Lion who is always on watch, rarely having to use his strength or tools to defend his cubs but always *ready* to do so. The lion only has risen and contributed a few times.

Directly behind me is my wolf. It is the fiercest of the beasts and the one I use the most when training. To attack a challenge the wolf is the first to step up.

If you want to up your intensity, go on Youtube and watch wolves hunt, then imagine you are one of them. What would you have to believe, see, think, and feel in order to have the fierceness?

To my left is a cheetah. I access the Cheetah for her speed when my heart rate spikes when running.

Behind the cheetah is a Gorilla, whom I access when I need pure power and strength.

When I need strength I will also imagine my kids taking over my body when training and gain energy from them.

These are mine, but yours can be much different. Do what feels right.

The last thing I want to share about your own personal mind gym is that there are surprises awaiting you inside there. I've had extraordinarily rewarding and spiritual experiences by utilizing this very special place. My brother Michael, who passed away before I was born, has visited me when I've pushed myself beyond anything I have done before and have called out for assistance.

There have been others as well.

Build Your Mental Toughness

In addition to the mind gym, you can take more steps to building out your mental toughness.

Start by reminding yourself that you've done it before.

List out 3-5 times you demonstrated mental toughness in your life. What was going on? When did these instances occur? How did you approach them? Who else was involved? What can you take from that time and re-apply or magnify in your life today?

You can also re-frame the problem, whatever it is that is, to make it feel more manageable. Use some of the techniques we described in Chapter 6 to shift your perspective of the issue and see if that helps.

Lastly, you can put your body and mind through a challenge. It can be anything, but here are a few of my favorites:

Run a Marathon

Meditate For 30 Days

Do a Positivity Challenge for 7 Days

SealFit.com has an outstanding 8 Weeks to Sealfit

Any challenge that requires you to dig deep, both mentally and physically, to meet the bar set in front of you. And you will do it, and the knowledge that you can will make you stronger as you move forward.

Of course, the same can be said of whatever challenge you're facing right now.

YOU'VE GOT THIS!

Chapter 17:

The Soft Side Of Success!

There is a side of success that is invisible. It shows up as our thoughts, feeling, prayers, intuitions, coincidences, gut feelings, ideas. Their "whispers" instead of "shouts," and if I were to leave them out of this book I would be leaving it incomplete.

I call this the "soft side" of Time Collapsing. Like much of this book, this is my "perception" as to how I see it and have experienced it.

The "Truth" About The Universal Laws Of Success

During a recent Thanksgiving, we took our kids to Dolphin Quest in Oahu.

Before they put us in the water, they did an exercise where they took a tuning fork and banged it off the ground.

Then, one by one, the trainer touched it to each kid's ankles and knees so they could hear the sound that the tuning fork could make.

They were demonstrating how dolphins could communicate. How they could see when completely blind folded and hunt using sound. They call it: "EchoLocation."

Echolocating animals call out to the environment and listen to the echoes of those calls that return from various objects near them. They use these echoes to locate and identify the objects.

Humans have a similar communication system with their thoughts, visions, questions, and emotions.

According to quantum physics, each of these has a real physical energy that goes out and attracts to it a similar wave. The higher energy and more focused your thoughts the faster those come into reality. The bad news is that if you radiate out lower energy thoughts and focus on them intensely, they will show up rather quickly and consistently as well.

I'm talking, of course, about the Law of Attraction.

It states that whatever you focus on expands and attracts that which is of the same energy level. The outer world is a mirror of your inner world, and whatever you consistently focus on will come into your life.

The Law of Attraction States: *belief that "like attracts like" and that by focusing on positive or negative thoughts, one can bring about positive or negative results. This belief is based upon the idea that people and their thoughts are both made from "pure energy", and the belief that like energy attracts like energy.*

How does this show up in our lives?

> We have all had the experience of thinking of a person and then that person calls us or sends us a message.
>
> Randomly a friend comes to mind, who you haven't spoken to in a year, then within a few hours you get a message from them.
>
> You have idea that you thought was completely new, but then all of a sudden you see it on T.V. or the Internet.
>
> Something tells you to NOT go down a certain street, but you do anyway, then get pulled over by a police officer.

You are experiencing a challenge, then randomly meet someone who is the exact person to help you with it.

These "coincidences" as we like to call them, are actually orchestrated events—whether by accident, or with purpose using the Law of Attraction.

I first heard this principle at the age of 22, when I stumbled across Earl Nightingale's audio course, "Lead the Field", then read his book: *The Strangest Secret.*

But "The Secret" has been around for centuries!

In the Bible, Jesus said, "Ask and you shall receive!" "The same that which is in me is also in you!"

In 1896, Ralph Waldo Trine wrote *The Vital Law of True Life, True Greatness, Power, and Happiness* *and "In Tune With The Infinite.* Then came *Universal Magnetism* by Edmund Shaftesbury in 1928. Napoleon Hill's classic *Think and Grow Rich* was written in 1937.

Then came Paulo Coelho and *The Alchemist.* And *Law of Attraction! The Basics of the Teachings of Abraham,* by Esther and Jerry Hicks. Rhonda Byrne's *The Secret* sold missions of copies and lead a huge surge in interest!

We have *The Science of Getting Rich* by Wallace Wattles; *As a Man Thinketh* by James Allen; *The Richest Man In Babylon,* by George S. Clason and *The Force,* by Stuart Wilde, to name a few.

As you can see, Law of Attraction is nothing new. The criticism is that you can't simply "think" of something and sit back and wait for it to appear. Yeah, no kidding. Isn't that why God gave us arms and legs? A mind to think, create, and share ideas to make our own lives better as well as for others in the world?

Earl Nightingale, in the *Strangest Secret* wrote:

Throughout history, the great wise men and teachers, philosophers, and prophets have disagreed with one another on many different things.

That is certainly true, and these books are no exception. It is only on this one point that they are in complete and unanimous agreement — the key to success and the key to failure is this:

WE BECOME WHAT WE THINK ABOUT

This is The Strangest Secret!

Now, why do I say it's strange, and why do I call it a secret? Actually, it isn't a secret at all. It was first promulgated by some of the earliest wise men, and it appears again and again throughout the Bible.

But very few people have learned it or understand it. That's why it's strange, and why for some equally strange reason it virtually remains a secret.

Marcus Aurelius, the great Roman Emperor, said: "*A man's life is what his thoughts make of it.*"

Disraeli said this: "*Everything comes if a man will only wait ... a human being with a settled purpose must accomplish it, and nothing can resist a will that will stake even existence for its fulfillment.*"

William James said: "*We need only in cold blood act as if the thing in question were real, and it will become infallibly real by growing into such a connection with our life that it will become real. It will become so knit with habit and emotion that our interests in it will be those which characterize belief.*"

He continues, "*... only you must, then, really wish these things, and wish them exclusively, and* ***not wish at the same time a hundred other incompatible things just as strongly.***"

My old friend **Dr. Norman Vincent Peale** put it this way: *"If you think in negative terms, you will get negative results. If you think in positive terms, you will achieve positive results."*

George Bernard Shaw said: *"People are always blaming their circumstances for what they are. I don't believe in circumstances. The people who get on in this world are the people who get up and look for the circumstances they want, and if they can't find them, make them."*

Well, it's pretty apparent, isn't it? We become what we think about.

A person who is thinking about a concrete and worthwhile goal is going to reach it, because that's what he's thinking about.

Conversely, the person who has no goal, who doesn't know where he's going, and whose thoughts must therefore be thoughts of confusion, anxiety, fear, and worry will thereby create a life of frustration, fear, anxiety and worry.

And if he thinks about nothing...he becomes nothing. **AS YE SOW — SO SHALL YE REAP"**

Psychologists say we have over 60,000 thoughts a day, and that 90% or more are the same thoughts from the day before. If we think about that in terms of pure energy output, that is a CRAZY amount of energy working at your service. When we think of it that way, it's easy to see why ***you will get in life what you put your thoughts, feelings, and intention.***

For the sake of having fun, let's pretend that the Law of Attraction is **1000% TRUE.** Fail-proof.

So, if these 60,000 thoughts are sending out signals and we are getting back exactly what we are sending out, wouldn't you want to take the first opportunity to step back and ask yourself:

"If I have total control and power to decide my thoughts—which dictate my destiny—wouldn't it make sense to determine what I want my thoughts to be?"

I can literally look back on my entire life and see the breadcrumb trail of how my thoughts lead to "coincidences" that led me to the next relationship or interaction that then gave me an idea, which then lead to the next big thing!

When we decided to move to the southside of Chicago. My wife and I wrote on a napkin the exact type of house we wanted with a ton of detail. What would our dream house have?

Then, literally the first house we looked at had every detail we put on that napkin!

You can put this to work for you! Every Time Collapsing Strategy, if followed, activates the Law of Attraction. Furthermore, by intentionally intensifying thoughts, feeling, desires, and then following up with putting action energy into the universe you SUPERCHARGE it!

"Ed, this is all B.S.! I've tried it and it never works for me!" I hear you saying.

The mistake most people make is that they hold Law of Attraction out like a sole strategy without realizing that it works in unison and as a collaborator with other universal laws.

Which leads me to The Universal Law of Expectation!

The **Law of Expectation states:** whatever one expects, with confidence becomes a self-fulfilling prophecy. When one injects with confidence the idea that good things are happening, they tend to happen.

On the flip side, when one expects bad things to happen they always do.

Will you always win? Will you always hit your goals? No!

We don't live in a perfect "outcome" based world. Meaning, just because you desired an outcome, does not mean you will get it.

However, we do live in a world that is putting us through a process, and by focusing on the process we ALWAYS WIN!

The paradox to this law is something called: **Law of Negative Planning!** There is a place for planning for everything that could go wrong. However, it must be done with the idea that "no matter what happens, we will prepare in order to make it a victory!"

So, you are using positive expectation in combination of negative planning as a way to actually build confidence. Our special forces say that one plan means no plan. You must always have multiple paths to winning.

Activate the Law of Attraction, add the Law of Expectation, and you'll be on your way—but the way you supercharge these is by adding the Universal Law of Gratitude.

The **Law of Gratitude states:** before the world will allow something greater into your life, you must be grateful where you are. You are where you are right now because that is where you are and you are thankful.

If you are in a tough place right now and you are listening to me talk about how you can direct your thoughts. You may be saying, "This all sounds good Ed, but you don't understand. I have all these problems."

Or, "You don't understand, I have the worst relationship, job, business, clients (insert whatever it might be)."

I hear ya, but listen very closely to the next line.

By continuing to "Yeah, but…" this principle you will continue to get more of what you are currently getting.

Your energy and your language will negate anything you have done with the Law of Attraction words.

When I was a kid, we didn't have a lot of money. My dad worked all the time so we had food on the table and clothes to wear, even if the majority of clothes were hand me downs. We always had enough.

As my mom would say when asked "Are we rich?":

"We are rich in love."

That sounded good to me. We felt that.

By finding gratitude in even the worse situations, you create an energetic shift that allows that event to move towards a better place.

When your body is stressed; your brain can't function like it needs to. By releasing gratitude, you begin a shift that allows you to find better answers, more resources, and better perspective.

Remember, by focusing on what "is," you continue to attract more of whatever that is. If you focus on it with negative energy, or an energy that is not what you want, you will create that as well.

Now, here's a great trick for getting out of that place fast: do gratitude stacking on yourself!!

Take five minutes and write everything you are grateful for.

If life sucks so bad that you can't, keep it simple. Write these exact sentences if you need to:

I'm grateful for my new awareness that my life sucks. (Or that it's amazing!)

I'm grateful that I can now direct my thoughts and begin the process of changing that.

I'm grateful that I have this book in my hand right now.

I'm grateful that I'm at the age of XX (insert your age) instead of 20 years down the road with this new insight.

I'm grateful that these strategies can create a new world for me.

Say this five times right now:

"All of Life Comes To Me With Ease Joy And Glory! How Does it Get Any Better Than This?"

- Dain Heer, Access Consciousness

Here is another statement that you can say:

I am Thankful for everything. Everything is here to support me. Everyone is cheering for me, whether they know it or not. I am destined to succeed and I was put here for a purpose.

Gratefulness ***IS*** the secret to raising your energy level, to moving from being a victim to taking responsibility. From "stuck" to expanded!

Now, if you are absolutely crushing it in your life right now, it is even more important for you to apply the Law of Gratitude as much as you can.

My kids and I love doing the grateful exercise when we are all together. When we say our prayers at night; the first line we say is:

"Dear God, Thank you for all our blessings..."

When you go to bed say: Thank You God, Thank You God, Thank You God.

When you wake up say: Thank you! Thank You! Thank You!

Without it, you are just going through the logical side of attraction and leaving out the energy vibration that REALLY starts the attraction principle. Which leads me to The Universal Law of Vibration.

The Law of Vibration states: whatever frequency you vibrate at, you will attract the same exact vibration. To understand this you must understand that everything has vibration.

The book you hold or iPad you read from looks and feels solid however it is put together by atoms that are moving at a speed so fast that it bonds together.

Thoughts are known to have a vibrational level that is higher than sounds, light, heat, and one that even today scientists are still studying and measuring.

Thoughts have creative power. Like magnets they will go out and get what you are focusing on... and attract MORE of it!

Therefore focus on what you desire, want, and intend to happen...as you will get them in abundance. Like seeds that you plant in a garden, if you nurture them and water them and get them sunlight, the only thing that can come out of that is the flower of the seed that was planted.

If you don't plant a seed of ABUNDANCE, Love, Positivity... then you allow others to plant their seeds in your garden.

Your "garden" is metaphor for you conscious, unconscious mind, and Super-Consciousness.

Taking Control Of Your Thoughts And Future Pull

If you allow people's negativity into your consciousness... then **you will get that.** You can look at the five people you spend most of your time with... listen to them for five minutes....and pretty much guarantee that you experience those same thoughts.

I call this the **Universal Law of Five People:** Your life, thoughts, and mindset will mirror the five people with whom you spend the most amount of time. You become a *by-product* of the people you surround yourself with, because their thoughts affect and infect your thinking.

There is an old saying, "If you hang out with four miserable and broke people..you are going to become the 5th."

You may think this is a joke, but it's the truth.

Who are you talking to weekly that is uplifting you? Encouraging you? Telling you that you can achieve your goals?

Who are you uplifting? Encouraging? Telling them they can achieve anything they set their mind to?

How do you want to feel? Do you want to have confidence, be positive, smile a lot, become an unstoppable person?

Then simply put ... surround yourself with five people that have these characteristics ... and refuse to spend any time or energy with people that are negative, losers, who are gonna put you down, themselves down, or others down.

Listen closely. I'm not joking when I say this.

If you are in a funk, or surrounded by pigeons who want to talk about the turd they are walking on, then the fastest way to change the energy pattern in your life is to surround yourself with a group of people who will support you.

Why do you think going to classes like Zumba, Pilates, book clubs, CrossFit, painting, photography, martial arts, or anything proactive is so uplifting for people?

In doing them, you are improving yourself *and also* surrounding yourself with people who have similar goals. If you try a group of people and it doesn't work...then try another one.

Another easy solution is to do what you are doing now: Reading a book on personal improvement and success. YouTube is great for this too! It's my go-to resource.

Yes, I need to feed my brain with awesomeness as well. I'm not immune to the silliness of negativity that is out there. I'll go to Youtube and put on: Wayne Dyer, Oprah Winfrey: Super Soul Sunday Clips, TED Talks, Tim Ferriss, Podcasts, Meditation Music, Stuart Wilde, or a SealFit video.

Here's why: *<u>your unconscious mind is "literal"</u>*... and when you allow bad energy or thinking from others into your space...or your garden... those seeds are getting planted.

An early mentor of mine, Tim Piering, wrote in his book *Mastery*:

"Where your thoughts go, energy flows, and results show."

Most people think of Law of Attraction as something that only focuses on thoughts. While this isn't entirely accurate, let's illustrate just for an example of the power of "stacking" strategies.

To **Illustrate:**

Thoughts --------> Energy --------> Results!

Napoleon Hill stated:

"**When your desires are strong enough, you will** appear to possess superhuman powers to achieve."

Listen to those words: **desire... energy......flow....superhuman powers**.

When you stack desire on top of it, does the energy go up or down?

I imagine desire to be emotion filled! Notice what happens to your body when you stop and ask these questions:

What am I inspired about?

What excites me?

What was my most heroic moment? When was there a time I could've given up, but I didn't!?

Who do I love in this world and intend great things for?

What else is possible that I'm not even thinking about?

Now, when you take those emotional states and pour them into your desire...you send into the world a new and amazing energy!

To Illustrate;

Thoughts -------->

Energy --------> Results!

Desire-------->

When you start stacking these exercises, results accelerate!

WHAT IS A DESIRE?

"Desire" is an emotionally placed thought based on what you intend to achieve, experience, change, or create.

By focusing on that desire intensely...you send out a supercharged message like a cellphone tower to all things, people, ideas, angels...and experiences to bring you there and them to you.

Now, if you want to take this to an entirely different level and completely separate yourself, you'll need to take Simultaneous and Massive Action!

The **Universal Law of Action:** movement with intention towards a strongly held desire to manifest followed by deliberate, focused, and relentless action in a short amount of time always brings faster results than inaction.

The Action is where your preparation is allowed to get tested, tweaked, and refined. It's where you, through experience, can constantly improve your skills, your message to the world, your artistry, your uniqueness.

None of those things happen by sitting and meditating alone. With that said, I will say that you can "attract" a LOT of amazing things through meditation. But to say you are prepared and aware of them when they show up is actually a different story.

That is why I'd like to share with you two more Universal Laws of Success:

ACTIVATING THE LAW OF ALLOWING:

When the very thing you asked for and thought about shows up, you need to be able to recognize it and happily say "yes" to it.

I'm a passionate guy who likes to work hard on the things I love doing, and do them at a word-class level if possible. That is why the law of allowing is one of the hardest ones to understand, get your hands around, and even tougher to get your mind around.

I find it's easier if I think about water.

ONE OF THE MOST POWERFUL FORCES IN OUR UNIVERSE IS WATER.

Water flows and goes where the least resistance allows it to go. When the opening arises it doesn't judge it, but it just flows in that direction and moves.

Humans don't do this. We tend to need to know logically "why" everything's the way it is and have a certain level of "comfort" or "certainty" before taking the next steps.

We are taught at a very young age to be cautious of anything we don't understand instead of being curious. When we have guessed or followed our intuition at young ages, we may have gotten in trouble or told to "show our work". Follow the "system."

As we got older, if someone offered us money or to buy something, our parents told us that it was inappropriate to accept for no reason at all.

This is where the **paradox of life comes into place.** You activate the Law of Attraction by putting your thoughts, your emotion, your questions, your actions into the world, but the receiving end of it means it's time to say "YES" to things that may seem to show up without any effort on your part at all.

I'd like to suggest to you that the universe is way more powerful than any "goal" you can set or "action" you can take. So, when you finally get into the "vortex," to use an Abraham Hicks term, the world starts to deliver what you asked for..or something better...or something that is in complete alignment with the energy that you have been putting into the universe.

When my kids jump on the trampoline, the Law of Gravity will pull them back down to the trampoline.

Wouldn't it be silly if they were upset about that concept?

Or, what if they were shouting "no" the entire time? That would be ridiculous right.

However, the world is working perfectly to support you and when great things show up in our lives it's easy to say; "No, I can't accept that!"

So, let me ask you a question:

"What have you been saying "No" to, either consciously or by accident, that if you started saying "yes" to it, would make your life so much more joyful?"

What if you stopped saying "no" and just said: "I am ready to accept and allow into my world all that you have ready for me!"

Oprah Winfrey and the Law of Surrender

In 1985, before Oprah was internationally famous and her show was just starting out in Chicago, she read the *The Color Purple*. She read the first lines of the book:

> "Dear God, I am 14 years old, please tell me what to do."

Oprah said to herself, "Oh my God, that is my story." referring to the young girl. "Someone else has my story."

When she found out that there was a casting call for the movie that Stephen Spielberg and Quincy Jones were producing, she thought it was a perfect sign. She started telling everyone that she was going to be in a movie. In her own words, "I have never wanted anything as much as the Color Purple".

She got a request to do a casting call for a movie titled: "Moon Song", but when she showed up to do the reading, she instantly recognized that it was the manuscript for "The Color Purple."

The best part, she was reading for a lead role, Sofia, who was married to HARPO. Oprah's name spelled backward! She thinks, "If that is not a sign from Jesus himself...I've never seen a sign bigger than that."

After months of not hearing anything, she decides to call the casting agent to see if there has been any update on the role. Instead, she was blasted by him, "Why are you calling me? I call you. I deal with real actresses. You have no experience."

Taken aback, Oprah believed she was not going to get the part. Sad, frustrated, and not understanding "why" God would play such a mean "trick" on her. She concludes that it must be because she is fat and sets off to a "fat farm" to shed some weight.

At the farm, she starts praying to God out loud:

"I don't get it. I don't get it. But I know you do. I don't know if this is some kind of joke. Or what you are doing with me. I thought you wanted me to have this part and I want to be in a space where I can thank you for the opportunity, but I can't. It's too hard. Please help me to let it go."

She starts singing out loud: "I surrender all, I surrender all. All to thee my blessed savior. I surrender all."

She repeated this until she could feel it lift, but didn't stop until she could say, "bless the actress who received the role."

Oprah continued, "In the moment that happened, someone comes running out to the track saying there is a phone call." It was Steven Spielberg letting Oprah know that **the role of Sofia was hers.**

In the video, which you can watch on Youtube if you search for "Oprah Surrender" she finishes with:

> "God has a much bigger dream than you could ever have for yourself. When you have worked as hard, and done as much , strived, tried, and given, and plead, bargained, and hoped... surrender. Give it up to that thing that is greater than yourself. Give it up to the flow. I have never wanted anything as much as the Color Purple.

"One of the fundamental turning points of my life was "The Color Purple". Nothing has had a greater impact on me, spiritually, emotionally, psychologically in determining my path!"

"The Color Purple is setting you up for the national Oprah Winfrey Show. I didn't know it at the time."

The Soft Side of success is the part that is hard to measure and quantify. It gets dismissed by many and oversimplified as well, but it's real.

Very real.

Chapter 18:

KINDNESS WORKS

I debated putting this very short chapter in, because I wasn't sure where it would fit.

Kindness is talked about in our schools, mostly referring to anti-bullying, but rarely discussed as success "tool". Many of the leaders portrayed in our society are of politicians. Sadly, this is very confusing and inaccurate for young people and aspiring leaders. Even worse, the level of hate that is being sent from one political side to the next is embarrassing.

If one would step back and look at it with common sense, they'd see that they are acting like idiots. My kids get stressed when the news is on and any politician is talking.

SIMPLE KINDNESS IS MISSING.

A new image of Success, one worth aspiring to, should highlight kindness as a core attribute that we acknowledge more often in public. The truth of the matter is: the majority of REALLY successful people are kind.

Success, fame, and money are simply magnifying glasses. If you are "jerk" before you have success, you will be one afterward. If you are kind early on, you will most likely be kind when you are "successful." Whatever that "success" means to you.

In sales, negotiating, business deals, marketing, competition, and yes, even in legal matters, you can choose kindness. Even if you don't want to do it for the other person, but ALWAYS do it for yourself. To protect your energy, consciousness, and way of behaving.

By designing your life, with many of the tools I've laid out for you in this book, you should have reversed the flow for everything to be moving toward you.

This does not mean that you allow yourself to be messed with, treated improperly, taken advantage of, or only do handshake deals. You still need to do your due diligence and utilize the tools that are there to protect you. You can have an edge in competition and still not be an asshole.

If you are ever in a situation where Kindness is not the best tool at your hand—examples would be: self-defense or handling a threatening situation—then do whatever you need to do, but promise yourself that you will do whatever it takes to stay out of that situation in the future.

Many of the toughest fighters, athletes, and entrepreneurs would destroy you in the arena, yet are the kindest people you'll ever meet.

Role models like Richard Branson, Peter Diamandis, Dan Sullivan, Vinnie Fisher, Yanik Silver, Jesse Itzler, Sarah Blakely, Oprah, Ellen, Jamie Foxx, Will Smith, Hugh Jackman, Justin Timberlake, and many of my close friends Matt Smith, Roland Frasier, Perry Belcher, Ryan Deiss, Lewis Howes, Tim Ferriss, and others are all kind people. My mom, dad, and wife are very kind people. In my eyes, they're also HUGELY successful.

We need more kindness in the presence of strength. And more strength in the presence of kindness. There is evil in this world and I wholeheartedly believe that we have warriors and are warriors to fight it.

Chapter 19:

THE PARADOX OF SUCCESS!

What you are chasing is running away from you...yet who you become will attract everything you want

There is an energy that I call "Chasing Energy." It exudes off people who feel that they don't have what they seek most.

WHAT THEY DON'T SEE IS THAT THEY ARE COMING FROM A PLACE OF LACKING.

Here are two definitions to clarify this concept of "Lack" vs. Abundance.

First, when a person is coming from a mental, spiritual, or behavioral place of "not having enough" they are coming from a place of "lack." This is not a literal concept, but one of mentality towards life or a specific context (i.e. work, relationships, family, money).

The main operating questions or statements a person who feels as though they are lacking may ask are:

- I can't get "x", because I'm too (insert the excuse: Fat, Slow, Short, Tall, Poor, Rich, Young, Old, Religious, etc..)
- Why don't I get the opportunity when person B just did and I'm better them him?

- My job/business stinks. My employees are clueless and lazy.
- The economy is crushing my business.
- I can't do "x", because I'm a single mom (dad, black, white, etc...)
- I'm too busy, overwhelmed, overworked, underpaid.
- My boss and the people I work with suck.
- If this doesn't work out, then I'm done.
- I'll do X (*write the book, start the business, get out of the dysfunctional relationship you are in, exercise, etc..)* next month, year, or someday.

As you can see, these questions and statement reflect a mentality that takes little ownership; it blames outside forces for the situation, justifies "why" this person got here and why they want to quit.

This plays out in all kinds of ways:

- I'll take this job today, because it will make someone else happy, and "hopefully they will give me a raise or opportunity.
- I need to build relationships w/ X person, because he or she will connect me. So, I need to kiss the ring...so to speak.
- I need to attend this networking deal because that is where all the players are going. I travel 20 weeks a year despite the fact I'd rather stay home with my family.
- Once I do "X", then I will be able to do "Y"...and then important people will want to work with me.

This energy is seeking approval, and no matter how "successful" you are, it puts you in a horrible position. I see it with people just starting out, as well as with people I would consider to be very successful in a LOT of areas of life. This lack mentality will attract more of the same kind of people that are resonating and living in agreement with that energy very rapidly .

I have been guilty of it so many times, and still need to catch myself whenever I feel like someone else has more or has it more figured out than me.

We need to flip this mentality on it's head. You may be asking, "Great Ed, but how do we do it?"

First, become aware of the feelings and thoughts/judgements you have in these key areas of your life: Relationships, Money, Family, Health, Spirituality.

How do you know you're struggling:

- You don't enjoy it.
- It's losing money.
- High customer complaints.
- You forgot what the purpose, passion, or truth that was behind your path...or there isn't one.
- You don't enjoy leading or driving the business.
- You have begun to resent it (this could be your business, a job, a relationship).
- There is friction! It's showing up between the owners, vendors, contractors, employees, and/or customers.
- Everything takes longer than it should.
- It feels heavy.
- When you see other people have success you resent it.
- When you see others fail you enjoy it.
- You are mentally working on the next business while "trying" to improve your current one.
- You put off what needs to be done until the last second.
- You think this will lead you to something better .

- You have been on the two-yard line for a long time trying to punch the deal through and it's not happening. "Time" is going by...but the "X" has gotten stuck.

We have all felt it, right?

Fortunately, I am NOT there yet with my current place. But if I reach it, I know I have what it takes to tackle the next pivot! How do I know?...

THE KEY QUESTIONS:

Do I have power and responsibility to control my future: income, time, relationships, place of living?

Have I discovered my own superpower, strengths, unique ability, accelerated learning?

What limiting beliefs have I accepted that are not mine?

My answers to the above questions are not yet obvious cries for change. There's another way I know, too: no one has shown up in my life looking to fix the problem.

When we're living in a state of lack, we unknowingly negate and push away everything that is showing up to support us. Instead, we attract people who are ready to "fill the VOID" or take advantage of an increasingly untenable situation.

Why?

Because when we're in a state of lack, we're expressing "need" to the world. Who shows up when you express "need" or a sense of "lack"? People who can capitalize off that situation. This could be salespeople, or relationships that appear to be exactly what you need in the beginning. However, it will turn out that your "lack" was fulfilling something in them...and once you solve it they will move on and leave you drained.

The key lesson is: **You can't ever expect a good high energy outcome to result from a low energy input.** It will never happen, unless it's purpose to wake you up and teach you about the path of no results or happiness.

LIVING FROM A PLACE OF ABUNDANCE

The opposite is also true and this is where an Abundant Mentality comes through.

An abundant mentality is one where a person always sees the blessing, amazingness, opportunity, possibility, and greatness in every situation, person, and result in life. By holding a fulfilled feeling when you set your intention of what you desire into the world, you will start to attract that into your life. By revving up the feeling that you will experience when you have already accomplished the goal or experienced the result, you rev up a "directional pull" that ONLY begins to bring everyone and everything that can support you.

The Abundant Life Starts Appearing Like This:

- People who want to help you for the good of everyone involved start showing up in your life.
- You start to find happiness and joy while doing what interests you most.
- Opportunities start showing up because you decide to follow your joy.
- Friends, Family, and/or other relationships that would suck your energy tend to stop calling or coming around. Your "light" keeps them away if they are seeking to experience more darkness or low energy.
- Your Intuition improves and you find yourself flowing with more harmony while noticing the coincidences of good that start showing up.

- The profession, the money, start showing up from places you didn't expect. It could be a raise, new client wanting something you don't offer, or a business opportunity that you never thought of prior.
- The relationships you build are ones of abundance. When YOU are doing good...it ONLY makes the relationship and life of all parties involved better because of your success. This is the type of relationship you want!

Now that you see the difference between the Lack and Abundance Mentalities, you might be wondering: why is it I can be making money, getting physically healthier, and seem to have the house I want, the family I want, and STILL don't feel like I'm "there" yet?

THE PARADOX OF LIFE

This is where life gets tricky.

When people accomplish the "goal" using the following classic formula...

#1: Set Goal

#2: Work Hard

#3: Attain Goal

...there is this idea that "I will finally arrive." **Attaining the goal feels like a destination, so once you "get there" you should feel happy and satisfied. That's just not realistic.** After all, life doesn't stop just because you achieved a goal!

If we see the goal as an experience that propels us into a new future of possibility and fun for our journey, then our feeling of happiness, confidence, and "I am there" will be a positive anchor.

Unfortunately, few people do this. **No one really teaches us that once we hit a goal a new "gap" is formed.**

Dan Sullivan, of The Strategic Coach, explains this gap as a never ending, always moving IDEAL. By the time you get to it, it seems to move off in the distance. It's like the horizon—as you drive towards the horizon a new horizon continues to emerge. Thus you never reach it.

Unfortunately, this leaves us always chasing it, yet never arriving.

Dan explains that most people live their lives with an idea that once they hit the "Ideal," they will THEN be happy. You see the problem with that thinking, right? Chasing horizons doesn't work!

I remember seeing a rainbow as a kid. It looked like it ended at just the next block over. When we ran to that block to find the pot of gold, the rainbow had somehow moved to the next block. So, we ran to the next block, but it was gone again.

If we "perceive" that the next accomplishment in our life or set of "perfect" circumstances will then fill the "it" that we are missing, we will be on a long never-ending road of always chasing something we can't catch. And THAT mounting frustration can throw our energy back down into Lack, attract low energy results, and trap us!

Think Winning Will Solve It

To give you a very specific example of this. Research shows that most Olympic athletes experience depression after they compete in the Olympic Games. Regardless of whether they win or not.

The imbalance of training required to be at that level puts so much more emphasis on that "goal of winning" and pressure on the athlete. If one puts so much pressure on this one leg of a four legged stool, eventually it will break. To see one event as the thing that will define you and make you "whole" is just setting you up for ultimate failure regardless of the results.

Think about it this way. Most professional and Olympic athletes hit their peak within ages 18-32. Imagine if the greatest thing you ever did happened when you were in this time frame and nothing in life could ever compare to that pinnacle experience.

Wouldn't the future of your life look bleak? Less bright?

Even if you had the brightest career ever, as time flies by we all end up at the end of it, looking back and reflecting.

If you don't have a strategy for defining the next IDEAL, minimizing the GAP, and a way of enjoying the PROCESS, you will always be chasing.

That is why your goal is to understand what the GAP is and what the IDEAL is...and how YOU have the power to manipulate them to serve you.

So, as you go for your ultimate goal of achieving a championship...you enjoy the process. Next chapter, we will deep dive into this, but we can't leave out the other big thing that most people are chasing: MONEY!

More Money Will Definitely Solve it! Right?

People who don't think money is important usually have more than they'll ever need, or they have none.

No matter who you are, money is an important tool in this world for creating the life you want to live. But does it create a sense of fulfillment and happiness?

I know a lot of guys who are high income earners, but are constantly chasing what they don't have. With no handle on life's process, they go from one thing to the next feeling as broke as they did the day before, despite whatever successes they accomplish.

Without a clear understanding of what will make you feel wealthy, happy and fulfilled, you are doomed to chase something outside of you like a hamster on a wheel...despite your ability to generate money.

You will always be on the "I'm not there yet" trap. Whether you have control over your income, profession, path in life...or not.

SO, WHERE DOES THIS LEAVE US?

Answer: in a really good place.

At least for the most part. What makes it tough is if we are stuck on the treadmill without any solutions, then we are now just aware of how stuck we really are. And if we were smart enough to learn how to conquer.....we are still screwed, because happiness eludes even the most successful among us without an understanding of how life's process works.

Here's why: once you make the decision to completely opt-out of the rules that trap the rest of our society, you no longer have to play by the rules common people live by.

To give an example:

If everyone has learned the "Sequential" way of thinking and living, we, as Time Collapsars use the Leapfrog Theory to leap to the top. Go straight to the front of the line...with zero time lag. No permission required.

If everyone is so distracted by the noise of life, they have lost their God-Given, Universal power to control and direct their thoughts, feelings, intentions and follow it up with purposeful action.

Stop and think about this!

If no one is doing this, because people are inundated with social media, facebook, cell phone, past failures, limiting belief systems, or they are achievers who keep falling into the void.....then listen closely.

As a Time Collapser, we see this VOID as an opportunity to inject our own intentions, actions, and desire to the universe and activate laws of attraction through our attention, focus, and intensity.

While life is just moving on for them, **it's unfolding for you.** With practice, you can steer this power that everyone has but don't use, and create the coincidences in your life and start lining up these superpowers while feeling abundantly wealthy during the journey.

While everyone else is *chasing* money... *chasing* people...*chasing* success...chasing happiness...we reverse it so all of **those things chase us.** This happens by deliberately defining a new way of defining wealth and happiness in your life.

Chapter 20:

THE GHOST OF YOUR PAST SELF

While we're on the subject of the soft side of success, the importance of kindness, and paradox of success, I want to talk about another trap that can appear once your Time Collapsing system gets to work in your life and you start seeing the exponential outcomes of your success.

It's when the ghost of your past self appears to slow your progress.

My first breakthrough for a client when I was working with a dentist who needed more dental implant patients. Since both my parents wore dentures, I ran over to their house and asked them why dentures sucked. I took my mom's biggest frustrations and wrote an ad that read:

"Attention Denture Sufferers!

FREE REPORT REVEALS How To End Your Frustrating, Ill-Fitting Dentures and Have Strong Teeth That Will Allow You To Eat Your Favorite Foods Once Again!"

The client ran the ad and generated $83,176. Not bad for an ad that cost him around $300! I immediately created more ads and marketing pieces specifically for attracting dental implant patients and launched another division within my dental marketing business. It was a seven-figure business very quickly.

FAST FORWARD NINE YEARS: Yesterday, I dropped my family off at the airport. On my way home, I saw an ad very similar to the one above. I had no emotion; only this thought: "Thank God I'm no longer in that business."

That guy who wrote that ad was a different version of myself—a ghost in some ways of a past life that has created a "pull" towards now. I appreciate who that guy was and the path that he walked, but I'm not that guy anymore.

All too often we can find ourselves haunted by the "ghosts of our past lives." The habits, beliefs, or thought patterns of these old versions of ourselves can sometimes be so ingrained that we can't see or feel their influence...or, even worse, we cling to them and resist change. Holding steadfastly to past and present may hold you back from your future. It can make it extremely difficult to embrace evolution, growth, and new directions.

In my businesses, I definitely see my own pattern of having excitement towards my work for a period of time, then a slow weaning off period until I'm ready for my next adventure. This can be really tough to do sometimes. For so many of us the question of "should I stay or should I go" on to the next chapter has become increasingly scary as life has grown bigger and louder with the responsibilities of caring for a family, mortgages, tuitions, false societal obligations, employees, and clients. Then there's the voice in your head that tells you: "I'M GOOD AT THIS..."

And yes, you might be very talented...but are you actually doing your best? If you are "staying" in something simply because you're winning at it, but you mentally have one foot out the door and one foot in.... THEN it's quite possible you are setting yourself up for a...

long,

slow,

frustrating,

road to inevitable failure.

What I mean by this is while you may still be better than most, if you're only sticking around because something comes easy to you, **people more passionate and less talented than you will outperform you!**

This is the consequence of holding on to the ghosts of our past selves. "And why is that?" you may ask. It is because our "ghosts" live as the finished identity of that point in our lives; they're a picture, and that image doesn't include the process it took to make them.

In other words, "Ed the Dental Guy" built a seven-figure marketing business. How many hours, fears, struggles, and setbacks did it take him to get there? *Eh, who can remember?* Our **ghosts make us forget the grind REQUIRED** to push the ball across the invisible line in order to go from non-success to success.

However, Time Collapsers understand they need to shed their ghosts, just like a butterfly sheds a cocoon. It doesn't have to be pretty, but it also doesn't need to be unnecessarily difficult.

Which brings me to this last point and how it relates to where you are going to inject your energy, passion, and life:

Once you find yourself unwilling, unwanting, or resisting doing THIS work...it's time move on.

The unwillingness to push your ball past the invisible line means it's time to focus on something where you are willing to do that. Because if you stay in something that no longer has purpose or spirit...you will be living the life of "The Ghost Of Your Past Self."

Chapter 21:

When Your Soul Awakens

So much of our life we are recognized for achieving steps up whatever ladder we might be climbing.

As I've taught throughout this book, you set the goal, you pick your model or mentors, you work to build your skills, and many times you reach your destination to find the "goal" wasn't what you really want after all.

Imagine if that ***realization*** was rewarded just as much as the achievement itself.

How differently would you feel about making the PIVOT from doing what you "thought" you wanted—and/or what others want for you—to go ahead and apply the process you learned to your next "path" of life.

I think I've made a professional career of "pivoting" and reinventing myself. Not intentionally though.

For me, personally, I love trying new things. I love learning new things. And thanks to the Time Collapsing process I've learned over the years to "test" something new is not scary.

However, knowing if the path you are going to test out is the "right" path, at a soul level, is a question I've been thinking about a lot lately.

In Wayne Dyer's movie: "The Shift,"[9] he opens with the poem from Carl Jung:

> ***"Thoroughly unprepared, we take the step into the afternoon of life. Worse still, we take this step with the false presupposition that our truths and our ideals will serve us as hitherto. But we cannot live the afternoon of life according to the program of life's morning, for what was great in the morning will be little at evening and what in the morning was true, at evening will have become a lie."***

Over the past few years, this paragraph has hit home to me more and more.

When I look back in my life, the "pivots" along the path are very obvious to me.

Getting my nursing degree, then abandoning nursing to pursue a motivational speaking career. Speak for a couple years, then pivoting into a info-publisher of mental toughness products, then pivoting again into becoming a marketing coach and consultant for dentists. Growing a very successful coaching business, and then selling part of it off 7 years later to once again venture out into a new field: the nutritional supplement business.

Expecting a fast and rapid success, I was shocked by the amount of potholes that awaited me, ready to suck up my dream of growing a successful product based company.

I stuck with it until I figured out how to grow the company profitably, and with the help of many good people made it a successful company. The lessons I learned were invaluable, but like previous businesses I had been a part of...it was what it was.

It allowed me the freedom to automate the marketing processes to create money while I exercised, grew our family from 3 kids to 7, ensured

---

[9] You can watch it at https://www.youtube.com/watch?v=K5O1CTlSwg4

I made every family event, and had loads of time to learn, and meet extraordinary people. Yet, even though we had great products, I didn't wake up with joy in my heart to expand the business... the message...the purpose.

I was just "doing" the job.

Why Do I Share All This Stuff?

There are so many amazingly talented, extraordinary people ***who are "stuck" in their success.***

Afterall, how could they ever leave?

This is how "The Success Trap" works...

You see what you think you want, you go out and conquer it, and you end up being on this thing called; "My Successful (insert your thing)".

This could be your business, your job/career, the person you are dating, the hobby you are mastering, the list goes on and on.

What happens is that there is now an obligation to continue your "success" as you and others now know it. Societal obligation will kill you if you don't get this awareness straight.

You build your thing...you now have a reputation and self-identity for being that "thing", people started treating you a certain way, **because of that "thing".**

Boom!

You are now molded...

To unmold something and resculpt is much more difficult than to just remain molded.

So, our society is filled with people who are trapped. Who are molded.

If you are a parent and have family obligations, you cannot take that lightly, however, you can build a path and plan from a soul purposed perspective that can serve you and your family in a greater way forever.

Maybe your job was to simply be a visitor on this path and you are ignoring your calling for something different.

To say "greater", better, or "something more" puts a judgement on that path, so I'll use the word "expand," because when your soul is awakened...*you naturally expand at every level.*

When you stay on a path you are no longer supposed to be on, you start to atrophy mentally, emotionally, and spiritually. It might not be noticeable to the outside world, because most of them are sedated by boredom, sameness, and the life hamster wheel.

Only a person who is living life from the core of their soul, an inspired life, will recognize when you make that shift...or that you have not.

It's easy to spot...very easy.

But not so easy when it's YOU going through the process of your soul talking to you. Or so covered and stuck in the "muck" of life.

My goal is to open a doorway that you can navigate your own journey, with your own rules, into living a soul-purposed life!

WHEN YOUR SUCCESS OR CURRENT PATH NO LONGER SERVES YOU

However, from a spiritual or soul level, the reason you may want to make the "Shift" as Dyer talks about. To embrace the idea Jung was trying to convey when saying that "***we take this step with the false presupposition that our truths and our ideals will serve us as hitherto.***"

Afterall this journey is one only you can do...and it is designed to allow you to create the life you were meant to live in a fluid way from a core level.

Why The Thing You Most Want...Is Avoiding You!

What you have been chasing has been running from you, because you chase it.

To think that once you "have" something, you can now BE something more, then you will be deserving of it. This formula is what our entire public process has been built on...leaving people feeling like someone else, outside of themselves has it figured out. This emanates an energy of "lack, not deserving, and not ready for the desider you are chasing.

Once you make this "shift" from no longer needing it...to already experiencing much more than that emotionally, mentally, and spiritually you begin to see everything you think you wanted plus much much more.

Roles have switched.

The thing **you were chasing is now chasing you.**

Happiness is like a butterfly: the more you chase it, the more it will elude you, but if you turn your attention to other things, it comes and sits softly on your shoulder.

- J. Richard Lessor.

This only starts to happen when you move from achievement focus to soul/spirit focused and Skillset Focused. When you start living from that place... my belief is that QUANTUM shift occurs. You now are ***THE*** magnet...without having to work as hard as you did.

It flows.

As Patanjali wrote: When one is Inspired by one great cause, dormant forces come alive.

A new sense of confidence emerges with a level of clarity that only you can see.

Conclusion:

DEATH AS AN ALLY

Bronnie Ware has a job not many of us would sign up for. She's a hospice nurse, who cares for those who have gone home to die. Over the course of her career, she was struck by how her patients came to find peace with the fact that they were at their end.

In her powerful book, *The Top Five Regrets of the Dying – A Life Transformed by the Dearly Departing,* Ware shares what she learned about life and living from those who were about to die.

REGRET #5: I WISH THAT I HAD LET MYSELF BE HAPPIER

Most people walk around with an idea that says, "When this happens, that happens, and then this other thing happens, THEN I'll be happy." They treat time as an infinite resource and happiness as a checklist.

I've got news for them: there's always going to be something out of whack. The question of whether that's a problem or not is how much focus you put on it.

I've met super wealthy people who have it all, yet they are not happy. I've met amazing people with more love in their lives to fill 10 cities, yet they focus on the one thing that isn't right. And they don't feel satisfied.

We are going to radically shift your thinking about this. You can't create something positive in your life when your focus is on something negative. As Wayne Dyer has said, "No amount of feeling bad will lead to good!"

We need a shift, people...and it needs to happen now!

REGRET #4: I WISH I HAD STAYED IN TOUCH WITH MY FRIENDS.

Creating and nurturing relationships that enrich your life, support you spirit, and make you better because you are in them is the secret to real fulfillment. It's really easy to get caught up in the details of work and life, and neglect the other relationships that feed our lives.

REGRET #3: I WISH I'D HAD THE COURAGE TO EXPRESS MY FEELINGS.

Many of Ware's patients lamented that they held back how they really felt about something in the name of keeping the peace. Their silence led to lost opportunity, long-carried resentment or bitterness, or even deep sadness.

Staying silent may have felt like the easier solution, but in reality it was a far heavier burden.

REGRET #2: I WISH I HADN'T WORKED SO HARD.

I don't believe people are afraid to work hard. In fact, most people are working way too hard on the wrong things. If you are passionate about something and feel it's what you were put here to do, then you happily embrace the work.

But there is a HUGE difference between working to further your passion and move your life in the direction you want and being on the treadmill.

REGRET #1: I WISH I'D HAD THE COURAGE TO LIVE A LIFE TRUE TO MYSELF, NOT THE LIFE OTHERS EXPECTED OF ME.

"This was the most common regret of all. When people realise that their life is almost over and look back clearly on it, it is easy to see how many dreams have gone unfulfilled. Most people had not honoured even a half of their dreams and had to die knowing that it was due to choices they had made, or not made. Health brings a freedom very few realise, until they no longer have it."[10]

When I look at that list, I see CLARITY. It's no easy feat to honestly assess where your life may have come off the rails and openly talk about where you feel your deepest pain. And those five regrets are crystal-clear insights made possible by the fact that these people had run out of time.

When it comes to Time Collapsing and achieving more than you ever thought possible, you have an unexpected ally in your corner: death!

DEATH AS AN ALLY!

The only time we ever talk about death is when someone dies, is going to die soon, or is sick. It's rarely celebrated and perceived as the inevitable powerful tool that we can use.

One core belief for taking total responsibility and having true authentic power is to USE all things in supportive ways. So, why not revisit the inevitable conclusion that we all are going to face?

What if you truly could live a life full of following your heart, filled with passion, and do not fear death, but better yet, use it to your advantage?

Sure, I'd love to live a long healthy life where I can watch my kids grow

[10] Ware, Bronnie. The Top Five Regrets of the Dying: A Life Transformed by the Dearly Departing. Hay House. Carlsbad, California. 2012

older and guide them, but I also would want my kids to know that I'm LIVING now. That this spirit inside of me is being expressed NOW.... and is not looking for permission to "start living."

If you remain in the traps of life, you will continue to seek certainty, before you are allowed to truly do what you want to do. The problem is that there is never a good time to break out and start living on your own terms.

Why do we have to wait for the inevitable reality that we are now older and time is limited?

A mom of a girl I coached told my wife and I, "The only regret I have is waiting til now to start doing things for myself. Now, the girls are out of the house and I don't know what I enjoy."

The Dalai Lama, when asked what surprised him most about humanity, answered.

"Man. Because he sacrifices his health in order to make money. Then he sacrifices money to recuperate his health. And then he is so anxious about the future that he does not enjoy the present. The result being that he does not live in the present or the future. He lives as if he is never going to die, and then dies having never really lived."

It's never too late to start living...and creating the life you want to live.

Start now and get moving!

URGENCY TO LIVE IS YOUR FRIEND

In Steven Pressfield's book, *Warrior Ethos,* he tells the story about how a Spartan warrior would rather die in battle with honor than to come back alive disgraced.

While walking this morning, I wondered if our society based our VALUE and "wealth" on whether we were living our passion or not.

If there was a way to measure the "ALIGNMENT" between the whisper in your heart and your actions in life. Of course, this is a personal journey that only you can take alone, however, it can be examined by sitting in silence and asking yourself, "Am I living in alignment with my spirit's calling?"

It seems we seek and await permission to be given to us before we can allow this part of our calling to be fulfilled. Yet, what if it was flipped, and we were actually pushed to live this type of life rather than one that has been outlined by our "traps."

Where we never seek society's criteria of success, but rather the one we discover on our own.

Where the true embarrassment of life would be to not live from this place...and honor and glory came to the person who led with their calling.....so when death came knocking, you could smile at it with full knowing you dominated life!

THERE IS NO SUCH THING AS DEATH

There is too much research and indications that show living on earth is just a pass through experience. We don't know if this is one life or if it's just an exercise to help expand your Soul's Journey!

A great book to read about this subject is *Dying To Be Me* by Anita Moorjani. She shares her story of having cancer throughout her body and dying. As she was dying, she floated above her body and could experience everything including the presence of her brother who was hundreds of miles away on his way to her.

She had a choice to stay in the light/heaven...or return to her diseased body. She chose to go back into her body...and in a matter of weeks she had spontaneous remission.

I tend to believe that we are here to evolve. To continually increase our vibration at a spiritual level, expand at the soul level, and to serve humanity by living our spiritual calling. Whether you want to call it life's purpose, Dharma, God's intention for you, or however you want to phrase it.

These are all happening simultaneously. It's not an either/or thing. However, if you are not living life from a place of passion you have a lower vibration. You're more prone to getting stuck in the emotional traps, societal traps, and mindset traps.

I'm not totally sure how this affects our evolution, but my perception is that life's "patterns" that end up teaching us lessons will keep showing up until we get it...and move on to the next thing. This is part of the evolution.

Say Goodbye to "I'm Too Busy"

You aren't too busy to live from your soul. You just don't know that it's okay to re-prioritize things. To delegate more in life. To say "no" more often to what isn't important.

As I get a little older, I am getting clearer and clear as to what types of conversations, people, places, and events bring joy and the ones that don't. This, I believe, is the ultimate point of Time Collapsing. Yes, the system will help you achieve more than you ever dreamed faster than you thought possible...but it will also redefine your reality from the inside out.

It will give you perfect clarity, not necessarily on where you're going next but on where you are currently. It will show you that true wealth and freedom are exactly what you say they are. And that success is something only you can define.

I want to leave you with some words from a poem called "The Invitation," by Oriah Mountain Dreamer.

It doesn't interest me
what you do for a living.
I want to know
what you ache for
and if you dare to dream
of meeting your heart's longing.
It doesn't interest me
how old you are.
I want to know
if you will risk
looking like a fool
for love
for your dream
for the adventure of being alive.

And finally,

I want to know
if you can live with failure
yours and mine
and still stand at the edge of the lake
and shout to the silver of the full moon,
"Yes."

Live BOLDLY! Embrace life so much that death is irrelevant!